A DIAMOND
IS A
DIAMOND

The Core Five Components to Social Justice

Sherard A. Robbins

Edited by Dr. Stephanie Troutman Robbins

Publisher: Independently published (December 17, 2019)
Language: English
ISBN-10: 1676413391
ISBN-13: 978-1676413394
Product Dimensions: 5.5 x 0.2 x 8.5 inches

Visceral Change, LLC
Tucson, AZ. 85716
www.visceralchange.org

Facebook: Visceral Change
Twitter: @Visceral Change/Robbins_MEd
Instagram: @Visceral Change
YouTube: Visceral Change

Our job as leaders is not to simply generate interest, but to cultivate opportunities and foster success, as well.

TABLE OF CONTENTS

Acknowledgements

The success of Visceral Change and the Core Five Components to Social Justice model would not have been possible without the support of the family, friends, and colleagues along the way. Chief of which being my wife, **Dr. Stephanie T. Robbins**, who gave her time and energy to serve as the editor of this book. She has been a champion of intersectional social justice for decades and continues to be one a driving force of the work.

Her knowledge and dedication as a professor and practitioner has touched the lives of many students, staff, and faculty worldwide and I have been more than privileged to have her in my life as my wife and my closest friend. Too, I want to give special thanks to the various mentors and professional partners who have helped shape and guide me on my professional journey towards justice: Daymyen Layne, Jesus Treviño, Laurie Lind, Jamie Utt-Schumacher, Hazael Andrew, Jay Carey, and Jamal Givens.

I would also like to also acknowledge Chopping Block contributing editor, Igna Gibson.

Equally important to our success are the challenges of life that spawn our many innovative and creative ideas. To those moments, I would offer that we try our best to show a level of patience and humility as I've learned that it is in those times that true character is being built.

Introduction

My Relationship to Social Justice

I consider social justice to be far more than a hot topic or a buzzword, I consider social justice to be a movement. As a definition, I consider social justice to be an intentional display of ongoing commitment where the objective is to create an equitable society for all citizens. However, one of the challenges with understanding social justice as a movement, ironically, is the misunderstanding of what is required of the movement itself. It is my belief that social justice is a linear process that is made up of three stages, *diversity, inclusion,* and *equity* (see Figure 0).

The first stage, diversity, addresses matters of difference. The second stage, inclusion, speaks to levels of involvement. Finally, the third stage, equity, aims to re-center the needs and necessities of those identities that have been traditionally and historically marginalized. The challenge the work of social justice is that most people tend to conflate the three stages, thereby using them interchangeably with one another.

As a result, individuals and organizations develop the belief that once they have accomplished one stage, i.e. diversity, then they have also accomplished the other, i.e. inclusion, and so on. However, in reality, to understand diversity is not to engage in inclusion, but to appreciate difference. Yet, we social justice educators know precisely that the acceptance of others must go beyond the optics of merely generating interest, as that is only the beginning. The next phase of work lies in the retention, support, and maintenance efforts applied to the diversity stage or initiative in order to accurately embark on a cultural shift. Once that is accomplished, entities can then transition to inclusion as inclusion speaks to involvement in ways that diversity does not. This level of involvement calls for the cultivation of opportunities that allow individuals to find purpose in their roles and their work, all the while feeling a sense of value as a result.

Finally, from inclusion comes a system and a practice of equity. This is re-centering the marginalized identities aimed at fostering success in fair and just ways personally, professionally, and educationally. This understanding of social justice anchors my *Core Five Components to Social Justice*, and it also drives how I position myself and the agency afforded to me within my intersecting identities as a Black man.

Agency is something I consider to be central to understanding and implementing social justice initiatives. Agency is an interesting concept for me because it has just as much to do with the consequences of a situation as it does the benefits. Once one begins to consider acting on one's agencies, one must also consider the consequences of those actions. What has been and continues to be most intriguing for me is that, in the context of the United States, I have the privilege and misfortune of living each day in one of the most dominant of identities and the one of the most subjugated of identities. Being a Black man means navigating the paradox of having access to masculinity while facing the oppression of racism. As a Black man, every day I have a decision to make with regards to agency, but that decision, at no point in time, can be impulsive or strictly emotionally driven; it must involve a *strategic* meeting with the mind. United States history has taught us the ways in which Black men have been problematized for centuries and it is the failure to address these harmful preconceptions/misconceptions that gives license to oppressors today. The very decision to enter a world beyond the safety of my home is coupled with great risk as the journey from home to work and back home again is not one to be taken for granted: as evidenced by the experiences of Black men from Medgar Evers to Henry Louis Gates and countless others.

This intersectional perspective allows me to better serve the essence of intersectionality, a term coined by the venerable Kimberlé Crenshaw in 1989. The term's genesis sought to complicate race and gender by bringing voice to the everyday struggles that Black women face(d) as a result of their intersecting identities when compared to White women (and other women of color). Intersectionality allows us to strengthen the conversations of race by demanding the discussions not be relegated to men or monolithic in any other way. Intersectionality allows us to recognize the challenges faced by Black men and women while creating equal space to identify and discuss the marginalization faced by the LatinX community and the Two-Spirited Indigenous communities, for example.

Another area of my social justice philosophy involves one's right to create space for free expression of identity. As a Black man, and from a Black perspective, this becomes critical because I've learned that the pervasiveness of anti-Blackness makes it difficult to find allies in this journey of self-actualization. I am fortunate because I am able, as a man, to enact my agency in ways that the system has not afforded to those whose primary identities are women (of color), folks within the LGBTQ community, and those who are disabled, to name a few. Operating within this area of privilege, it is important for me to create and shore up opportunities that allow people from marginalized groups to have a platform for expression in any way that I can.

Thus, it is because of my lived experience in a marginalized identity that I approach social justice from a critical perspective. James Baldwin once said, "I love America more than any other country in this world, and, exactly for this reason, I insist on the right to criticize her perpetually." As a social justice trainer and a lifelong learner and educator, it is important to me that systems of oppression and marginalization are acknowledged in general society before moving onto establishing wider efforts for diversity and inclusion. It is only through a keen understanding of the Core Five Components to Social Justice that the unilateral and perpetual support and integration of diversity, equity, and inclusion can be achieved.

My Professional Perspective
Higher Education

Organizationally, I have been privileged enough to initiate many diversity and inclusion programs and strategies in an effort to advance institutional culture. At two separate institutions, I have championed Men of Color initiatives that focused on retention and success of young men of color enrolled at Predominantly White Institutions. Through this effort, I helped create a nationally recognized program at one of the most prestigious Research 1, Public Ivy institutions in the country.

At a different Research 1, Public Ivy institution, I oversaw a diversity office of Equity & Student Engagement which, between the center itself and the staff, served as a five-time award winning university entity. In leading this office, I was tasked with creating a team at the grassroots level that would go on to inspire change and cultivate multiculturalism through the campus and community.

Finally, in 2018 I served as the Team Lead for the inaugural National Inclusive Excellence Leadership Academy; a 5-week intensive institute created and executed by a man I consider a mentor of mine, Dr. Damon Williams. I was honored to be chosen with such responsibility and to work with a trusted team of Coordinators, Directors, Associate Vice Presidents and Vice Provosts to discover a way to decentralize diversity for a major institution.

Visceral Change

Through Visceral Change, I have been able to engage diversity and inclusion in very challenging and effective ways. Our organizational development engagements include working with major non-profits and top colleges, universities in the United States, as well as many premier international institutions and organizations. As the founder of Visceral Change, I took it upon myself to create, among other things, a Social Justice Institute. This intensive day-long/retreat-styled training institute is preceded by an online training module that introduces participants to the concepts and key terms of the institute. From there, participants will receive a certificate symbolizing their completion of the training institute.

Other areas of Visceral Change's work include, but are not limited to: training and development workshops, coaching and advising, strategic planning, and overall organizational development. Annually, I, and my staff and contributors, present groundbreaking content at various national conferences throughout the country. I also created "The Chopping Block," an interview series that highlights many local, regional, and national diversity and inclusion educators and leaders.

In sum, centering social justice as the impetus for my work has proven to be purposeful for me. It allows me to engage people in ways that position critical Whiteness, toxic masculinity, heteronormativity, ableism, and other dominant-centered identities as a means of understanding the context behind the imperialist capitalist White supremacist patriarchy, as my dear friend Dr. bell hooks names. What is true is that I view diversity, inclusion, and equity as more than just pillar areas for organizational development – for me, they are basic necessities for everyday life.

Looking Ahead

This book, in its essence, is designed to serve as a guide for individuals, groups, and organizations who are looking to better understand social justice and the components from which the concept derives. *A Diamond is a Diamond: The Core Five Components to Social Justice* offers a first-hand look at the Core Five Components; a model I designed and theorized in 2016. These components, Power & Privilege, Identity & Intersectionality, Systems of Socialization, Cultural Competence, and Allyship & Advocacy, serve as the foundations that make up the work of social justice. My aim is to help individuals and organizations confront the conflation between diversity, inclusion, and equity, en route to understanding the work that encompasses the larger movement of social justice.

The Core Five are predicated upon rectifying this conflation and seeks to challenge the sense of normalcy the misconception brings. Encouraging readers and participants to "disassociate in order to dismantle," I provide new ways for individuals to begin thinking about diversity and inclusion as a means to impact themselves and their organizations at large.

What follows next is a two-tiered approach to the Core Five Components to Social Justice. Grounded in data and research, this guidebook is designed to (1) aid others in their personal journey towards understanding social justice and (2) to help cultivate a more socially just and equitable workplace. Each goal is achieved by providing the reader with tools and examples of how to confront their own implicit biases, stereotypes, and perceptions of certain traditions and cultural norms. Supported by numerous articles, authors, and supplemental references, the Core Five Components to Social Justice will help you shape your life and your organization in a more inclusive and equitable way.

A Journey Towards Social Justice

Diversity	Inclusion	Equity
…is Difference	…is Involvement	…is Re-centering
…is generating interest	…is cultivating opportunity	…is fostering success

Figure 0. Visceral Change

PART 1:

THE CORE FIVE COMPONENTS TO SOCIAL JUSTICE

CORE FIVE COMPONENT #1:

POWER & PRIVILEGE

A DIAMOND IS A DIAMOND

Component 1: Power & Privilege

We begin our Core Five Components to Social Justice with an examination of power & privilege. I view this component as the starting point because in our exploration of social justice work, privilege, most specifically, serves to anchor the concept in ways that the other four components do not. For example, when we delve into identity and intersectionality, we will learn about the ways our identities shape how we view the world and, equally, how the world views us. However, the perspective from either side has almost everything to do with the ways in which privileges have been associated with our prescribed identity. It then becomes a question of whether or not we are innately privileged as people, or if it is actually our identities that are privileged as a result of their position in society. In order to understand social justice as a whole we need to first understand the concept of privilege, and the best way to foundationally understand the concept of privilege, is to begin by exploring Dr. Peggy McIntosh's Five Pillars of Privilege (1992).

Five Pillars of Privilege:

Over her prestigious and storied career, Dr. Peggy McIntosh has worked diligently to understand the various aspects of privilege. As a White woman, she understood that she experienced life in a way that was largely privileged, but also marginalized at other times. In her effort to make sense of why her privilege seemed to be contextual rather than constant, she crafted the following five pillars:

A DIAMOND IS A DIAMOND

1. Privilege is a special advantage; it is neither common nor universal.
2. Privilege is granted and bestowed, not innately natural.
3. Privilege is a right or entitlement that is related to a preferred status or rank.
4. Privilege is exercised for the benefit of the recipient and to the exclusion or detriment of others.
5. Privileged status is often outside of the awareness of the person possessing it

(McIntosh, 1992; Robinson & Howard-Hamilton, 2000)

I do not disagree, for example, with Dr. McIntosh's pillars of privilege, in fact, I quite agree with them. I do think, however, they need to be contextualized in order for practitioners of social justice to fully grasp her position. McIntosh's Five Pillars, at first glance, may read as if they have sort of a "both/and" requirement, however, they function better when read as if they were independent of one another. In other words, privilege can either look like pillar #1 _or_ pillar #3, for example, and not necessarily all five absolutely. Let's break them down:

Privilege is a special advantage; it is neither common nor universal

Privilege, in its very essence, is not something that is ubiquitous nor is it something that we, as individuals, necessarily share with the person or people to our right or to our left. For example, we understand that, in the context of this country, men are granted far greater privilege in the working world than their women counterparts. This is evidenced by the steady gender pay gap in the American work force. According to the American Association for University Women, "in 2016, women working full time in the United States typically were paid just 80 percent of what men were paid, a gap of 20 percent" (www.aauw.org). The AAUW went on to state:

> The gap has narrowed since the 1970s, due largely to women's progress in education and workforce participation and to men's wages rising at a slower rate. Still, the pay gap does not appear likely to go away on its own. At the rate of change between 1960 and 2016, women are expected to reach pay equity with men in 2059. But even that slow progress has stalled in recent years. If change continues at the slower rate seen since 2001, women will not reach pay equity with men until 2119.

This example clearly illustrates that the privileges granted to the average working man in the United States of America are not granted to women. These privileges provide men with a special advantage, oftentimes leading to greater means of wealth, as well as influence in the workplace.

A DIAMOND IS A DIAMOND

Privilege is a right or entitlement that is related to a preferred status or rank.

Privilege can manifest in the form of a right or entitlement courtesy of one's order in society or within a general hierarchical structure. Though not necessarily guaranteed on a macro level, when condensed, it becomes very easy to identify where certain privileges are granted and for whom they benefit. For example, the wealth gap in the United States has been a problem for decades and even centuries. In 2018, the United States of America has a population of approximately 327 million people; of those 327 million, the average household income hovers at approximately $68,828.00, according to a marketwatch.com study (www.marketwatch.com). In order to be classified as the "top 1%," the same study showed that a household income would have to average approximately $421,926. Market Watch also found that the top 1% of Americans took home more than 22% of all income in 2015; that's the highest share since a peak of 23.9% just before the Great Depression in 1928.

This example harkens back to privilege because we know that the more money one makes, the more opportunities one has. One of the ways that opportunities are measured is through the idea of legacies, and the main way legacies are formed is through wealth attainment (the value of your assets minus the value of your debts). Christopher Ingraham, columnist for the Washington post wrote that "the wealthiest 1 percent of American households own 40 percent of the country's wealth…"

A DIAMOND IS A DIAMOND

(www.washingtonpost.com). With this number being the highest it's ever been since 1962, the author continued to add that:

> From 2013, the share of wealth owned by the 1 percent shot up by nearly three percentage points. Wealth owned by the bottom 90 percent, meanwhile, fell over the same period. Today, the top 1 percent of households own more wealth than the bottom 90 percent combined. That gap, between the ultrawealthy and everyone else, has only become wider in the past several decades.

The statistics presented by Market Watch and the Washington Post indicate the ways in which privilege tends to benefit individuals who are of certain wealth. The opportunities that are afforded to those who average a household income of $421K are oftentimes nothing more than a fantasy for those who rake in $68K - which is a very honest salary - further creating a separation of wealth and power in the United States.

The working and poor classes, however, very really find themselves afforded the opportunities to participate in the discussions about wealth unless it's a matter of acknowledging the important role they play in capitalism. Too, these statistics do not disaggregate for race, ethnicity, and immigrant status - another conversation all together.

A DIAMOND IS A DIAMOND

Privilege is exercised for the benefit of the recipient and to the exclusion or detriment of others.

In a world where binaries and dichotomies are being challenged more than ever, there is at least one area where the conversation of extremes is still accepted universally - privilege. It is true that there are many shades of grey whenever we talk about contexts and structures that are made by and for the people, however, when we talk about systems that advantage and disadvantage, then we realize that one person or group's benefit is to and at the detriment of another's.

White privilege, for example, is arguably the greatest privilege one can have in the world, certainly in the United States. In fact, according to teachingtolerance.com, "white privilege shapes the world in which we live — the way that we navigate and interact with one another and with the world" (www.tolerance.org). Yet, it is important to realize that White privilege is most stark when contrasted with anti-Blackness.

Looking, again at the United States of America, the historical representations, for better or for worse (though, largely for worse) of White privilege and anti-blackness are not effectively measured when independent from each other. History has taught us that the darker one's skin was, the more inferior and subordinated one became. Suzanne Forbes-Vierling, columnist for Medium.com wrote that "...white slave owners preferred Africans who possessed

A DIAMOND IS A DIAMOND

European features" (www.medium.com). Vierling, in her same article, also found that:

> Research on colorism indicates that racism exists and delineates the benefits of light skin privilege, even to the point of equating it to the power of male patriarchy and white feminism. It can't be denied that colorism gives some black people advantage.

These examples highlight the ways in which Whiteness through skin privilege, specifically, is to the benefit of whiter-skinned people (i.e. White or light skinned) *when compared* to darker skinned individuals. We know that this unfortunate reality has a home in the United States' adoption of chattel slavery, a system that relegated all Blacks to involuntary servitude, but was especially cruel and unusual to the darker skinned Africans.

Privileged status is often outside of the awareness of the person possessing it

Privilege is oftentimes most prevalent and most hazardous when it is unconscious. Unconscious privilege can oftentimes lead to unconscious bias, which can cause us to act in ways that are harmful to other people. Most often, unconscious privilege, though harmful, is not dangerous in the same ways unconscious bias has proven to be. For example, unconscious bias can lead to the unfair and unfounded stereotyping of marginalized groups, ultimately resulting in something disruptive or even fatal (*See State of Florida v. George Zimmerman*). Unconscious privilege, however, tends to further promulgate the marginalization of identity groups (in problematic ways, at times), but generally does not result in anything too extreme. For example, Christian privilege in the United States is so ingrained in our society that it not only affords certain religious groups time off from work, it calls for mostly everyone to have time off from work, regardless of whether or not they celebrate the holiday (e.g. Christmas); yet, holidays like Hanukkah and Mawlid-al-Nabi are not met with the same national and societal respect. A 2015 article in Everyday Feminism stated that:

> Although the holiday season makes Christian privilege a little easier to notice, the real problem goes far beyond nativity scenes and Santa Claus. Christian privilege rests on the idea that Christianity is superior to other faiths and to atheism and humanism.
> (www.everydayfeminism.com)

Christian privilege, in essence, is the religious *and* societal privilege that is afforded to Americans that allows us to expect to have time off to celebrate the holidays, regardless of our religious affiliations. The Everyday Feminism article said it best when the writer said, "Conflating holidays like Hanukkah with Christmas not only erases their actual

26

significance for the people who observe them, but also reinforces Christian privilege."

"A Diamond is a Diamond"

You'll note that I have yet to mention Dr. McIntosh's second pillar, *Privilege is granted and bestowed, not innately natural.* That is because I was saving this one for last. Dr. McIntosh's second pillar is one that is very near and dear to me because it serves as the influence for the very book you are reading. If I were to ask you to think about a diamond and to share with me what things you associated the word with, what would you say? Chances are you would associate a diamond with words such as shiny, or wealth, or power, or beautiful. These, and similar words or expressions, are the responses given by almost every person I've asked to answer this question; even though we all know that a diamond in its truest form is really none of the above.

This is because once we consider the realities of a diamond, we realize that it is merely carbon - a piece of the earth; pressurized rock. Thus, this begs the question, *"why are these responses not the first ones that come to mind when asked to describe a diamond?"* The answer is simple: it is because we've been conditioned, or, socialized, to associate diamonds with sentiments of luxury and opulence, even if those associations are not indicative of what a diamond in its truest form really is.

A DIAMOND IS A DIAMOND

In other words, a diamond is just a diamond unless value is put on it; and the irony of this statement is that the same holds true for the concept of privilege. White privilege, male privilege, class privilege, religious privilege, heteronormativity, and any other forms of privilege one can think of are all products of social conditioning.

Disassociate in order to Dismantle

There are many ways to go about disrupting the systems of power and privilege, or as I say, *disassociating in order to dismantle*. If we accept that a diamond is a diamond, then we can begin to view the intersections of power and privilege systemically as a way to *disassociate* ourselves from the identity in order to *dismantle* the stigma. The first way is to acknowledge the we have privilege. Much like anything we try to combat that we find troublesome or problematic, it is always most important to acknowledge the topic of concern.

This not only aides in identifying the problem outright, but it also helps us to identify the problem in all of its forms (e.g., racism, sexism, homophobia, islamophobia, etc…). For example, as a Black man in the United States, the level of oppression that I face based on race is frequent and often. However, oftentimes whenever I am in a leadership position and partnered with a White woman (e.g., giving a presentation or a training), the attention of the room is always directed to me. This is because, even though my race is oppressed in the general American and global contexts, my maleness carries the weight of the privilege in reference to leadership and success.

The reconciliation for most racists becomes, "well, if he's in a leadership position, then he must not be like the *other Black people;*" and for them, that is reason enough. In other words, so long as the representative is not a woman, the image can remain preserved. It is important for me, then, in such circumstances, to use the privilege afforded to my maleness not only redirect the attention of the room to my female counterpart, but to also take a secondary position, if possible, in the presentation or narrative. This understanding of the ways race and gender intersect is what would allow me to disassociate in order to dismantle.

The reason, one would argue, Anonymous circles always begin with the individual sharing their name and their addiction is to get the problem out in the open; I think it is fair to say that the addiction (and/or its benefits and advantages) to privilege is a real thing. Acknowledging one has privilege can be achieved, for example, by thinking critically about the social systems and structures to which one belongs.

Privilege, as Dr. McIntosh states, is to the benefit of some and to the detriment of others; that is, to the benefit of dominant identities and the detriment of subordinated ones. In other words, if you are benefitting from societal privileges, chances are that not only might this be unbeknownst to you, but you might also be ignorant to the harm your privilege is causing others. A true *ignorant bliss*, one might say.

Thinking critically about the social systems and structures to which one is bound would allow one to take a tertiary position on issues of inequities and effectively identify the ways in which one contributes to them via one's own privileges. This position would also demand that dominant identities, such as those of wealthier backgrounds, place a conscious effort into considering issues of privilege instead of taking the path of least resistance – that is – deflecting responsibility onto the already marginalized group or individual in consideration. For example, even with an understanding of the capitalism and the way it operates, it is common practice for the rich and wealthy to place blame on the working class and the poor for their socioeconomic circumstances, rather than finding ways to use their money to contribute to a more equitable standard of life.

By doing this, the wealthy do not trade in their value nor do they give up their positionality in the hierarchies of society, instead, they become active participants in a solution oriented approach to the problems of capitalism and systemic disenfranchisement. The idea is that one would gain a clearer understanding of how systemic oppression operates at a larger level. For example, according to the 2017 U.S. Census, as of July of that year, Black Americans made up 13.4% of the United States (www.census.gov), yet, as of 2018, they make up 38% of America's prison population, as reported by the Federal Bureau of Prisons in an August study of that year (www.bop.gov).

A DIAMOND IS A DIAMOND

With these comparative figures being as galvanizing as they are, at some point in time even the most racially privileged individual would have to question the statistics. As a result, the privileged yet reasonable and rational thinker should conclude two things: (a) that all Blacks are not, in fact, criminals or destined for criminality, and (b) that it is true that there is a larger systemic issue at hand.

Another way we begin disassociating in order to dismantle demands that we learn to listen. When someone confronts us about our privilege, we need, to listen in the moment and evaluate the ways their feedback is actually helpful. We must then reflect and integrate that information into ow we receive and react in conversations about diversity, equity, and social justice.

McIntosh states that privilege is oftentimes outside of the awareness of the beholder, thus, it is not farfetched that the microaggresed might identify one's careless use of privilege before the actual microaggressor. If this is true, then so is the possibility of not recognizing one's privilege and, as a result, it becomes important that we listen to the ways in which we can and must improve.

A common response may be to try and explain our actions away by becoming defensive or making jokes. For example, if a heterosexual person is confronted about their insensitive behavior or comment about the LGBTQ community, the individual might respond by saying, "Oh, relax, my sister is a lesbian!" or "it's okay, I know tons of

A DIAMOND IS A DIAMOND

gay people!" The truth is, it's not much of a joke if only one person is laughing.

Embracing Discomfort

Embracing discomfort is part of the journey to all forms of self-discovery. When confronting privilege, specifically, it is of utmost importance that we each become comfortable with getting uncomfortable. Confrontation, like any challenge, requires bravery and courage. The courage to stand up for one's beliefs as well as the courage to take chances and risks. South African Archbishop Desmond Tutu once said, "if you are neutral in situations of injustice, you have chosen the side of the oppressor." Leaning into discomfort and actively engaging in the disruption of harmful normative systems is at the root of allyship and advocacy.

For some people, this means doing individual research on systemic issues such as why the Dakota Access Pipeline controversy of 2016 was such an important issue, and for others it simply means speaking up on behalf of those less privileged when they aren't necessarily the ones being affected and, therefore, don't entirely have to. In either instance, social justice asks that each potential ally and advocate find courage in moments of discomfort and to become brave in the face of confrontation. When we take opportunities to challenge systematic oppression through easing into the unease, we contribute holistically towards a more socially just world.

A DIAMOND IS A DIAMOND

Throughout one's journey to recognizing privilege, the roadblocks and speedbumps will appear very real. In many of my conversations with people of dominant identities around the topic of privilege, many of them tell me outright that they don't want to have the conversation because it is difficult to hear. More than that, however, are the people who have a misinformed understanding of what privilege is.

Privilege, by loose definition, just means that there are things in this world we don't have to worry about if we don't want to – especially if they don't negatively impact our day-to-day life. For example, as a man, society affords me the privilege to not worry about women's issues if I don't want to as the outcome does not directly impact my personhood. The same goes for my other dominant identities, such as being able-bodied and heterosexual.

In my experiences, however, most people miss that definition of privilege and sooner assume that the word is associated with a life that lacks work ethic or one that benefits from the spoils of wealth. 'Privilege,' in short, harkens to the advantages one receives as a result of a particular identity. That identity, however, determines how much, if any, privilege one is afforded in their specific context, or in society. Because privilege is largely contextual, it will not be until we can view the concept systemically and as a social construct that we can begin to fully commit to a worthwhile examination of the topic.

CORE FIVE COMPONENT #2:

IDENTITY & INTERSECTIONALITY

A DIAMOND IS A DIAMOND

Component 2: Identity & Intersectionality

Identity and intersecting identities play a major role in the ways in which social justice is understood, depicted, and even received by people. After all, they are, for the most part, the thing(s) that give us purpose and meaning in life; Identities are directly linked to privileges in that they are the vehicle where by privileges are conferred and received. In other words, some identities, like Whiteness, come with privilege, access to opportunities, and other unearned advantages.

Identities bestow and withhold privilege according to their value within our social orders, cultures, and communities. Thus, in this section, we will explore the concepts of identity and intersectionality as they relate to power, privilege and the benefits one does or does not garner as a result of them. We will discuss how systems have long-since played a major role in privileging our identities, but in order to effectively understand the ways in which systems of privilege benefit certain identities over others, we must first understand exactly what I mean when I say one must *disassociate in order to dismantle.*

The Relationship Between Privilege and Identity

You see, when we think of those most fortunate, that is, those individuals who live privileged lifestyles, we tend to think of these people as inherently privileged. We tend to forgo the notion that these individuals have benefitted from a system that has been designed to support their identities and instead, we implore that these individuals, by way of nature's design rather than society's, are privileged – and that's just not true. We must remember that privilege is not neutral and that it is ascribed through careful designations that are and have been socially conditioned and reinforced.

It is imperative to understand that we, as people, are not innately privileged, but rather, it is our identities that are. For example, when we challenge someone regarding an ideology or position we may believe is the result of privilege, we always, for the most part, inform the individual of their privilege in one of two ways: by saying that they are *privileged*, or by indicating that one of their *privileged identities* is responsible for their ability to engage in their course of action. No person ever means it literally when one calls another individual *"privileged."*

One does not believe, even on a subconscious level, that an individual, inherently and in one's soul, is privilege personified, but rather, one will believe that something about an individual (in this case, their identity/ies, or some aspect of it/them) is privileged. For example, it is not Nick, the White man from Boston, Massachusetts who is privileged, but rather, it is the white skin that Nick wears, which receives benefits from the social power structure, that allocates privilege and value to Whiteness.

Furthermore, it is Nick's *unchecked relationship to Whiteness* that results in the promulgation of privilege in the form of conscious and unconscious discrimination (such as racist behaviors, etc…). Conversely, I, the Black man, am not afforded privilege through my Blackness and, thus, cannot engage racism in the same way that a Nick can. By understanding the relationship between privilege and identity - that is, how identities are influenced by privilege - we can begin critically discussing the ways we can unpack the social influence that constructs dominant and subordinated identities.

In a five-week intensive social justice training, I collaborated with my good friend and fellow diversity consultant, Jamie Utt-Schumacher, to engage a largely White audience on the concept of Whiteness. In his workshop, Jamie introduced a three tiered approach to Whiteness: White Culture, Whiteness, and White People (Utt, 2018). His position was that no White person by nature is inherently racist.

He concluded that, were this this the case, then there would be no hope for redemption and the concept of allyship would cease to exist. Instead, Jamie argued that it is one's relationship to Whiteness, in this example, that causes one to be racist, but that in challenging this level of conditioning, one can evolve beyond racist action and ideology. Another colleague, Dr. Nolan Cabrera, covered one week which focused on the history of Whiteness and detailed the foundational context to Whiteness and its relevancy in a national and global context.

As a rule, if we can begin to view our identities as privileged, then we can begin to disassociate from the benefits we received as a result of our privileged identities, in order to dismantle the social structure that gives them power. In other words, we can move beyond the fallacy that we, as people, are innately privileged, and begin to understand that it is our identities that privilege us. This shift in comprehension will also allow us to cease personalizing particular comments – the *micro* - and help us to truly view certain themes from a larger, broader perspective – the *macro*.

Privileged Identities

In the context of the United States of America (but *certainly not* limited to it), there are a set of identities that receive privileges, or advantages, in ways that other identities do not. In much of our social justice discourse, we tend to discount the notion of a binary, but in the topic of privilege, I would argue that the binary (though not absolute, necessarily) is alive and well. Where men are advantaged in the social hierarchy of society, women tend to be disadvantaged. Where American citizens are met with privileges as a result of their nationality, immigrants and other folks who naturalize are often met with a sense of inferiority due to the lack of privilege that society places on those identities. Here, Dr. Peggy McIntosh's pillar holds true that to every advantaged identity, there is a disadvantaged identity. Figure 1 provides examples of some, but not all, privileged and unprivileged identities.

A DIAMOND IS A DIAMOND

Privileged Identities	Unprivileged Identities
White	People of Color
Male	Female
Heterosexual	LGBTQIA+
Upper-Class	Lower-Class/Poor
Ability	Disability (varying degrees)
English Speaking	English Learning
Two-Parent Household	Single Parent Household

Figure 1

To reiterate, this list is by no means exhaustive, nor is it intended to be, but I think one thing we can conclude form this list is that the relationship between privilege and identities is most evident. Too, it is true that there are some shades of grey that exist even within the privileged/unprivileged binary. For example, with respect to identities that are disadvantaged when it comes to privilege in American society, the opposite of heterosexually identified people (*privileged*) is not necessarily gay or lesbian identified people.

The LGTBQ Community acknowledges a spectrum of identities that are similarly marginalized, such as those that are bisexual, gender fluid, gender non-conforming and transgendered. And within the LGBTQ spectrum of identities, each individual experiences marginality differently than the next. That is, a lesbian, by virtue of being a woman, will almost certainly experience discrimination due to her gender and sexuality whereas a gay man may experience only discrimination due to his sexuality. Similarly, a transgendered person will likely experience a level of discrimination in ways that cis-gendered gay and lesbian men and women will not, however, transgendered people of color statistically experience more discrimination and danger than the larger spectrum altogether.

The oppression one faces in society as a result of identifying within the LGBTQ community is generally uniform with respect to the feeling of not-belonging, and so a sufficient antithesis to heterosexual identities that gain privilege would be the acknowledgement of the LGBTQ community as a whole (though there is stratification even within this community).

To find examples of the ways in which identities are privileged, you need only revert to the examples of privilege illustrated in the first component of the Core Five. However, in an effort to help my readers make sense of the ways in which identities are privileged, I want to introduce two concepts I call, Micro-Awareness and Macro-Awareness. Micro and Macro-Awareness refer to the ways in which we, as individuals, receive the concepts of privilege as it relates to our own lived experiences. Oftentimes when we explore the concept of privilege, we tend to absorb the information in ways that make sense to our individual lived experiences, and not in ways that consider the larger sense of systematic oppression.

A DIAMOND IS A DIAMOND

Micro-Awareness

Individuals who tend to lack a true understanding of privilege are often viewing it through a subjective lens and understanding the information on a micro level. One's micro-awareness of the information generally causes the individual to deflect from larger concepts that would connect one's identities to the privilege. As a result, that individual begins to develop barriers designed to focus on their specific lived experience(s), ultimately ignoring the larger system of oppression from which they benefit.

For example, in the circle of dialogue produced by my training sessions it is not uncommon to hear men or male identified participants finding difficulty grasping the experiences of the women or female identified counterparts. When a female college student shares that she is uncomfortable walking back to her residence hall at night by herself, the male college student tends to ask "why?" Even after the woman shares and contextualizes her fears of possibly being attacked on her journey back to her room, it is still commonplace to find the men respond by saying, "I don't get it? I walk that same path to that same hall and I have no problems."

The reason why the male students in this hypothetical (yet, very realistic) situation are unable to understand the women's struggle is because the male privilege that is afforded to their male identities (in conjunction with their developmental level around the topic) has initiated a state of micro-awareness that has caused them to personalize the information. Too, the constant state of "normality" surrounding these men is one that places maleness and masculinity at the center. As a result, men, and other dominant identities, find it difficult to intellectually understand experiences that are not theirs because, quite frankly, they don't have to. The design of the social system is such that the dominant identity holders are not affected negatively by the challenges faced by more subjugated identities.

Macro-Awareness

Individuals that are able to understand the very nuances of privileged situations and the privileges afforded to those identities are likely receiving the information on a macro level. Individuals at this stage require less coaxing and do a better job seeing the larger systemic issues that often spark social movements and initiatives. One's macro-awareness of the information suggests that a person understands that situations of privilege, direct or indirect, are in fact a privilege that is afforded to their own (dominant) identities.

For example, the White individual who is in a state of macro-awareness will be able to understand and articulate the reason for the disproportionate minority confinement in the United States. Where research illustrates that in the average lifetime of a Black man, 1 out of every 3 will either be killed or in prison (Kessler, G. 2015), the macro-aware individual will recognize that, although that may not directly contribute this statistic, they still benefit from it (because of the particular relationship their Whiteness has with the situation), and, thus, the reality of the circumstance is not to be dismissed.

It is important that I reiterate the critical element that founds the essence of disassociating. By asking folks to disassociate in order to dismantle by entering a stage of macro-awareness, I am not offering exemption to oppressive ideologies, approaches, or behaviors. What I am suggesting is the need for us to constantly keep our dominant identities in check as a way to challenge the discriminatory behaviors society has given them grace to conduct. Residing in a place of micro-awareness makes it easy for individuals to address issues that are directly in front of them, but it also makes it difficult to understand the systemic issues that ground them.

Each of us have a series of intersecting identities that serve to both, marginalize and privilege us depending our identities' relationship to society in that circumstance. As an extension of an earlier example, it is not that all men are sexist or toxic in their masculinity, it is that all men and benefit from a level of male privilege (in the context of this society) that allows them to behave in sexist ways with relative immunity. For men of color, it is true that their lack of skin privilege does not afford them advantages in that regard, but their maleness and masculinity still holds beneficial rank in society.

Where it is true that macro-awareness allows an individual to make sense of the larger systemic connecting oppression to privilege and identity, that awareness by itself is not enough. The next stage would require the individual to regularly challenge their behaviors in an effort to take responsibility and remain cognizant their life-long growth and development process.

Intersectionality

Before speaking about intersectionality and how it's used in its current context, it is important that we first acknowledge its derivation. We must remember that the term 'intersectionality' was coined by Kimberlé Crenshaw, a Black feminist professor at Columbia Law School, as a way to acknowledge the intersections of race and gender as a grounds for discrimination against women in the workplace (Coaston, J. 2019). What began as an acknowledgement of shared-identity oppression has quickly burgeoned into a term where its significance now resides within its ability to capture and corral identities that exceed race/gender and that its endurance lies within its capacity to surpass its legal usage. This evolution, of course, has not gone unnoticed by Professor Crenshaw, in fact, one would even say she's greeted the reframing of the term with arms wide open. In a write up on the Columbia Law School's website, Crenshaw is quoted as saying:

> Intersectionality is a lens through
> which you can see where power
> comes and collides, where it interlocks
> and intersects. It's not simply that
> there's a race problem here, a gender
> problem here, and a class or LBGTQ

44

problem there. Many times that framework erases what happens to people who are subject to all of these things. (Crenshaw, K. 2017).

Intersectionality is important because it frames one's experiences in a way that allows for the questioning and critiques of multiple power structures. In her Ted Talk of the same name, Professor Crenshaw explains Intersectionality by recognizing that what we once may have thought to be sheer racism we now know is also met with sexism. And in an effort to disassociate in order to dismantle, the ability to critique socially oppressive systems through the lens of intersecting identities is absolutely fundamental.

Although intersectionality was coined to highlight the oppression of multiple marginalized identities, specifically as they relate to race and gender, we see that the term itself has been harkened in reference to other identities, as well. In fact, one of the more profound examples of how societal standards of acceptable intersecting identities has problematized a person is in the narrative of Tonya Harding, the (in)famous Olympic-class figure skater of the early 1990s. Older readers may remember Tonya Harding from her high-profile rivalry with Nancy Kerrigan which ultimately saw Harding banned for life from the Olympics. Younger readers may have seen the movie *I, Tonya* which provided insight as to how the bludgeoning of Kerrigan's knee came to fruition.

Although the movie and rivalry was completely centered around the Kerrigan/Harding rivalry and Harding's subsequent involvement in the assault on Nancy Kerrigan, what the movie also paid attention to were the ways in which Tonya Harding was treated (for the majority of her career) by Olympic judges and the media because of her socioeconomic status as a poor or lower working-class White woman.

In its incipience, Kimberlé Crenshaw coined the term in order to foreground the ways in which oppressive systems impact different identities in different ways, specifically highlighting the areas of race and gender in relation to Black women. Over the years, this term has been expanded and applied to include all identities/aspects of identity. Oftentimes intersectionality is decoupled from its core principle (which is the acknowledgement and critique of oppressive systems in relation to women of color), however, it remains intentional about highlighting some of the more challenging areas multiple, diverse (and marginal) identities can cause people.

While the term has traveled and morphed in useful ways; Crenshaw's most recent work using intersectionality involves the hashtag **#sayhername** which centers Black women's experiences as victims of police brutality and law enforcement violence.

It is through a firm understanding of social identity and intersectionality that we begin to recognize how the power given to them impacts us as people. We learn to recognize that, for example, if Bob, who is White and Christian, is Islamophobic or exhibits Islamophobic behavior it is likely not due to Bob being a bad or inherently racist person. More than likely it is a combination of his relationship to Christianity and a nationalist ideology that emphasizes the image of terrorism as someone who identifies as Muslim. This way of thinking is critical to one's ability to challenge the social power bestowed upon identities in an effort to engage in the discussions around isms and normativity more productively.

CORE FIVE COMPONENT #3:

SYSTEMS OF SOCIALIZATION

A DIAMOND IS A DIAMOND

Component 3: Systems of Socialization

Socialization, or, social conditioning, is one of the lesser noted aspects of social justice. This is ironic because, through much of our discussions around concepts like privilege and identity, we tend to always come back to this question of how one attains a certain racist or homophobic state of mind in the first place. The answer to that is simple: it is because we have been conditioned by a set of influences, both internal and external (i.e., family, environment, media, etc…) that have socialized us to view groups and ideologies in a particular way.

Using religion as an example, my brother would always say, "One is not born religious, but rather, one is born *into* a religious household." In other words, unlike the human fight or flight response, religious ideals are taught and learned over a period of time. One learns how to be a Christian the same way one learns ow to be Buddhist – through knowledge acquisition, traditional norms and behavioral repetition; and we know that anything learned can be unlearned. Similarly, this logic applies to all areas of socialized concepts as we will explore in the following paragraphs.

An Exercise in Socialization

In an exercise as part of my Visceral Change training workshop, I ask the audience to mentally remove themselves from the room by either closing their eyes or diverting their attention elsewhere. With their eyes closed, I ask them to picture, in succession, first an American without context and then three Americans with context; that being a nurse, a housekeeper, and an inmate. Upon opening their eyes I ask them to share aloud a detailed description of what their Americans looked like (height, race, gender, hair color, ethnicity, etc...), and it is always amazing how similar the responses are, regardless of age, generation, or identity groups.

What generally happens in this exercise is the brain begins to play on its biases, both explicitly and implicitly. Defined as "a particular tendency, trend, inclination, feeling, or opinion, especially one that is preconceived or unreasoned," biases seek to take these unreasoned or preconceived notions and normalize them as a part of one's every day experience.

For example, when imagining a housekeeper, I've noticed that most people picture a Latina woman, older, with brown skin. When confronted with why this particular description of an individual entered their minds, most folks explain that their description is a mere reflection of either their own experience with housekeepers or the ways in which the media has portrayed housekeepers on television or in movies.

James Baldwin eloquently describes a similar example of socialization in his famous debate against William F. Buckley where he said:

> In the case of the American Negro,
> from the moment you are born every
> stick and stone, every face, is white.
> Since you have not yet seen a mirror,
> you suppose you are, too... It comes
> as a great shock to see Gary Cooper
> killing off the Indians, and although
> you are rooting for Gary Cooper, that
> the Indians are you.
> (www.nytimes.com)

It is also true that in this exercise, participants struggle to remain honest in their vulnerability. More often than not, participants will conjure of an image that matches the stereotypical image of the housekeeper or the inmate, but they will then change their image on the spot. Some participants have stated that, by changing the image, they felt better about themselves. Although this may be true, what is most important to note is that their initial image remains their primary response, triggered by their implicit bias.

The Process of Socialization

Herbert Spencer (1898) refers to socialization as the process of inheriting and disseminating norms, customs, and ideologies; and albeit this theory is dated by over a century, the premise is still widely accepted today even by me. What's most unique to me about Spencer's theory is his decision to use the word "process" when describing socialization. I say this because the word "process" suggests something that is learned overtime, or, nurtured.

We tend to accept much of the things attributed to socialization as natural or even absolute, and unfortunately, a lot of the time those things we accept are harmful. For example, one's belief that certain races are inferior or more prone to violence than others can be extremely damaging to those groups being targeted. The statement alone should be dismissed at prima facie, yet, there are thousands, if not millions of people who believe this to be true. This is because these individuals have been socialized to believe there is truth in these statements.

Dr. Zimbardo's infamous 1971 Stanford Experiment examined the ways in which human socialization manifests itself in a room full of strangers and with little direction (www.prisonexp.org). Folks familiar with the experiment will remember the ways participants took on the rolls of both, prisoner and officer, but what was most interesting was the participants' decisions to behave in accordance with how they understood a prisoners and officers to act in that particular context.

In his book, *The Lucifer Effect: Understanding How Good People Turn Evil*, Zimbardo (2007), a world renowned social psychologist, explores the age-old question of whether or not humans are evil by nature; he posits:

A DIAMOND IS A DIAMOND

> Most of us know ourselves only from
> our limited experiences in familiar
> situations that involve rules, laws,
> policies, and pressures that constrain
> us… But what happens when we are
> exposed to totally new and unfamiliar
> settings where our habits don't
> suffice…? The old you might not
> work as expected when the ground
> rules change. (p. 6)

The truth in Dr. Zimbardo's postulation about how we respond to a situation is very accurate, but by itself it is incomplete. For example, it is true that we are adaptable by nature, and as a result, are forced many times to adjust to the ways in which we see the world. But what about the ways the world sees us? If it is true that we as people will inevitably adapt to adversity, then is it also true that there is single solution for all people to overcoming such challenges? My answer, and the answer of many of my compatriots, is no.

One message I try to encourage my audience to heed when working with the behaviors and actions of individuals from differing identities is the understanding that *We all struggle equally, but our struggles are not the same.* What this means is that, I believe that there are some uniform life experiences that the vast majority of people share. For example, when speaking about struggle, one can justifiably assume that most people have experienced a bad relationship or break up, or that most people have been in poor financial standing.

However, what one cannot do is treat the specific identity struggle of a group as uniform. That is, the Black struggle in America, for example, is not the same as the Asian or Pacific Islander struggle in America. Similarly, the Lesbian, Gay, and Bisexual struggles in America are not the same as the Transgender struggle.

The Problematization of Black Communities

The points aforementioned are best articulated when we consider the systemic impacts of how socialization is often designed to villainize certain identity groups. For example, in one Visceral Change training session, I make a point of saying to my audience "If I'm going to war, don't give me an explosive or a firearm, don't give me a sword or a knife - give me the system; because if I can control your image, I've already won."

What I am attempting to emphasize here is the old adage that perception is reality. I attempt to convey to the audience that the truth matters, but only to the people who want it to. To many conscious educators and advocates, there is a very real and very legitimate explanation for the school to prison pipeline that we find in communities of color. While to others, it's easier to believe that the large number of people of color in prisons is more accurately attributed to their proclivity to violence or lack of intelligence.

A DIAMOND IS A DIAMOND

The unfortunate truth about the adage is its accuracy, as the ideology has harmed Black men and women in American society for centuries. If a Black man is killed in the streets or murdered by a cop, many people react in the same manner they do were he a Great White Shark, with a sigh of relief, as if to suggest that the threat had been neutralized – regardless of context. This would also explain why officers, for centuries, have been cleared by the judicial system even in light of their unlawful actions (see Philando Castile, Sandra Bland, Freddie Gray, Tamir Rice, and so many others for examples).

In an article titled *Joe McKnight and the Fear of the Black Man*, Martenzie Johnson examines the cause for Black men and women being killed – with relative immunity – by White people. He says, that it is "because the idea of a black man being a law-abiding citizen is a form of cognitive dissonance. Which is why a law like "stand your ground" was never intended for African-Americans, and why the National Rifle Association is reluctant to defend the rights of all gun owners" (Johnson, M. 2016). He goes on to state that, "Zimmerman, unknowingly, designed a playbook over four years ago that plays off that fear of blacks for the benefit of white Americans..."

It is this socially accepted belief that people of color are inept that permits a level of clemency to certain groups for such heinous acts. The thought that a Black professor like Henry Louis Gates, erudite as he may be, could actually live in a specific sect of Cambridge, Massachusetts (as he had for years) is preposterous to some White people and serves as a basis for why he "must have been" in the wrong.

We understand that the system that drives economic success and ostensible American idealism is not one that centers those of us who experience life on the margins. As a result, the exclusion of marginalized identities from much of the "American Dream" is, both, an intentional and unconscious objective.

CORE FIVE COMPONENT #4:

CULTURAL COMPETENCY

Component 4: Cultural Competence

Hailing from Boston, Massachusetts, I confess that I have been known to be a little more direct and assertive than most people I have come to know. It could have been my birth into the Commonwealth or the 27 years I spent grooming myself in the ways of the state's cultural norms that caused me to be such a way. Let me be clear, I don't mention any of this to suggest that I am ashamed of who I am as a result of my birth, growth, and development in Boston, but really to illustrate how my Bostonian experience made me who I am today. In fact, it wasn't until I moved to North Carolina that I became aware of my person as it related to how I dealt with other people. Not only was I told that my accent was thick, but I was also told that I was intimidating. One could argue that race played a factor in this belief, but a large part of it, too, was also my upbringing.

The truth is, the cultural norms associated with what it means to hail from Massachusetts or to be Bostonian have been instrumental in my character development. To know Boston is to know me as to know me is to know Boston. In other words, in order to understand me and what it is that I bring with me to the spaces I occupy, one must first have a level of competency in what it means to be from Massachusetts; but of course, this is just one finite example of cultural competence.

A DIAMOND IS A DIAMOND

For many people, cultural competency is something that is viewed on an extreme, that is to suggest that either one has it or they don't. The problem with that approach is that it negates the fact that competency, in all forms, is a process of development; and development is always on a spectrum. As a result, cultural competency has become a term that we hear quite often in the DEI world, yet, one that is often veered away from in practice. In some instances, people will shy away from engaging in a difficult dialogue due to the fact that they don't have an in-depth understanding of the topic, while in other instances, people will disengage because they don't agree with the discussion and find it unnerving or uncomfortable. In either case, discussions of competency need to be met with patience and practice as it is important to meet people where they are in order to get them to where they need to be.

Proving Competence

To be (or to become) competent in culture, specifically outside of your own experiences and identities, is critically important to the establishment of a socially just world. Cultural competence speaks not only to the ways in which one can gain a sound, keen understanding of the world's identities, but it also seeks to provide one the tools necessary to practice humility in the face of other identities. The process of becoming culturally competent, though, is not something that is met with instant gratification; after all, we must remember that cultural competence is directly linked to the systems of socialization that govern the ways we view the world to begin with. One of my favorite examples of this comes from the historical event that was the 2016 Presidential Campaign, and though I could focus on Donald Trump as a way to highlight some of the dangers of cultural *in*competence, I am actually thinking about Hilary Clinton in this example.

During her campaign, Hilary not only ran as a Democrat, but had relatively sound and documented progressive ideologies that supported her liberalized approach to the White House. However, in 1996, the then First Lady made a comment on at Keene State University labeling gangs of kids as "super-predators,' saying, "They're not just gangs of kids anymore, they are often the kinds of kids that are called super-predators – no conscience, no empathy…" (C-SPAN, 1996).

I reference this moment in Clinton's political life because what she viewed as appropriate and *normal* in 1996 came back to reflect negatively on her exactly two decades later. Many Clinton critics, specifically those of color, were apprehensive of supporting the candidate in 2016 simply because they were not convinced that she had grown past this belief of hers.

It is important to note that the critics of this comment were people of color overwhelmingly) because it was clear to most diversity scholars and critical race theorists that the very language used by the First Lady that referenced "gangs" and "drug cartels" was not meant to reflect the affluent White neighborhood in the Foothills. This critical yet justifiable challenge to Senator Clinton's perspective (years later) displays how the affirmation of a culturally competent person can only manifest after one has demonstrated effectively (and to the approval of the marginalized) that they have or are willing to change. While Clinton did acknowledge that her 1996 comment was flawed and apologized for it, many saw this as insincere, too late, or not enough. The reversal of cultural incompetence or lack of cultural awareness takes a sustained commitment to actionable efforts for equity and change.

Equally important to note is the fact that not all cultural identities are visible. If we think of cultural identity as an iceberg, we learn that there are some visible components to culture that allow for one to formulate assumptions based on their understanding (through socialization) of what is in front of them. Too, we learn that there are some cultural identities that lie below the surface and are not as easily identifiable or discernable to an individual, even through our assumptions and perspectives.

For example, we can look at an Indian woman wearing a sari or a Middle Eastern man wearing a turban and begin to assume (rightfully or wrongfully) some form of cultural association, specifically that of either national or religious affiliation. However, by simply looking at someone, it would be far more difficult to assume, for example, the gender role one chooses to practice in society, or their parenting style. The distinctions between Surface Culture and Deep Culture play an important role in how we understand cultural identities and culture-based identity

61

practices. Cultures have an enormous amount of influence on behavior and it is important to have a clear understanding of how culture impacts the things that we say and do.

Cultural Humility

As aforementioned, Cultural competence is an essential aspect to social justice. It is a powerful tool that effectively ties our actions to our thought processes. It is what allows us to fully comprehend and appreciate the differences in each of us, both, individually and as a group, as well as understand the various ways privilege benefits certain groups to the detriment of others. However, cultural competence without cultural humility can be very dangerous.

In an article published by the American Psychological Association, Amanda Waters and Lisa Asbill (2013) define cultural humility as the "ability to maintain an interpersonal stance that is other-oriented (or open to the other) in relation to aspects of cultural identity that are most important to the [person]." They argue that it is beneficial to understand cultural competency as a process rather than an end product as a way to leave room for what Tervalon & Murray-Garcia, (1998) call a lifelong commitment to self-evaluation and self-critique.

Cultural humility asks us to be humble in the presence of other cultures, especially when reflecting on the challenges each culture faces. Through cultural competence, we are able to use our knowledge of other cultures for good or for worse. For example, if I am competent in what words hurt or serve as emotional triggers for other cultural identities, then I then have the power to exact myself in such a way that is harmful to these groups or people. Conversely, cultural humility calls for us to recognize the damages of such term and actions and to find ways to serve as allies rather than oppressors in the work of equity and equality.

Being uninformed about the invisible parts of culture can lead to misinformation, stereotyping and if not careful, marginalization. If we are going to become more culturally informed, we must first take the time to get to know the whole person. This will give us a greater understanding why people react a certain way in situations as opposed to others.

Bias and Behavior

Part of what makes the work of cultural competency difficult stems from a concept known as bias. The sociological definition of bias suggests a tendency (either known or unknown) to prefer one thing over another that prevents objectivity, influences understanding, or impacts outcomes in some way (www.sociologydictionary.org). Allow me to begin with an illustration. The University of Arizona gathered excerpts taken from *Hidden Bias: A Primer*, an article published by Tolerance.org, in an effort to provide resources for understanding Bias and behavior. What the article found was that:

- Unconscious beliefs and attitudes have been found to be associated with language and certain behaviors such as eye contact, blinking rates and smiles.
- Studies have found, for example, that school teachers clearly telegraph prejudices, so much so that some researchers believe children of color and White children in the same classroom effectively receive different educations. Similar results have been noted with regards to students with disabilities and LGBTQ students (Crumpacker & Vander Haegen, 1987; Shapiro, 1999).
- Studies indicate that African American teenagers are aware they are stigmatized as being intellectually inferior and that they go to school bearing what psychologist Claude Steele has called a "burden of suspicion." Such a burden can affect their attitudes and achievement.
- Similarly, studies found that when college women are reminded their group is considered bad at math, their performance may fulfill this prophecy.
- Integration, by itself, has not been shown to produce dramatic changes in attitudes and behavior. However, when people work together in a structured environment to solve shared problems through community service, their attitudes about diversity can change dramatically.
- Imagining strong women leaders or seeing positive role models of marginalized peoples has been

shown to, at least temporarily, change unconscious biases.

It is my belief that cultural incompetence, along with the ways in which we are socialized, serves as a foundation for the biases that we hold as people, about other people. Bias effects how view difference. Addressing bias, however, is not a one-time commitment that produces instant gratification. We must remember that committing oneself to challenging biases must be accompanied by a commitment actively and ongoingly engage with critiquing and challenging systems.

It is important that we remain open-minded when it comes to other cultures and that we lean into discomfort when growing in diversity; in other words, if we want to change we must not only accept but embrace the notion of becoming comfortable with being uncomfortable. Examining our biases is a good starting point for moving toward cultural competence.

CORE FIVE COMPONENT #5:

ALLYSHIP & ADVOCACY

A DIAMOND IS A DIAMOND

Component 5: Allyship & Advocacy

At this point, I would like for you all to reflect on the founding principle that governs my LLC, Visceral Change, and our work with diversity & inclusion. Visceral Change at its very core is rooted wholeheartedly in the belief that no one can effectively act as a social justice advocate, ally or change agent for someone else (or on behalf of a cause) without first acknowledging and understanding the ways in which they themselves show up to or in a space. This premise around self-awareness is the foundation of all of the diversity and inclusion work that we do.

Each of us need to be keenly aware of how our identities—and the privileges afforded and ascribed to those identities, shape and challenge the very spaces we occupy in community with identities outside of our own. As we think about the evolution of the Core Five Component to Social Justice, from Power and Privilege to Cultural Competence (Components 1-4), we realize that the next logical step, after awareness and knowledge acquisition, is practice/praxis. This step involves actively participating in social justice advocacy work. The first thing we must recognize is that allyship and advocacy, albeit similar, are not the same. They overlap and are interrelated, but *allyship is to the individual or group while advocacy is to the cause.*

Allyship

Suffolk University defines an ally as "a person who is (oftentimes) a member of an advantaged social group who takes a stand against oppression, works to eliminate oppressive attitudes and beliefs in themselves and in their communities, and works to interrogate and understand their privilege" (www.suffolk.edu). What is clear about Suffolk's definition of an ally is that there is a specific focus on the self, and where allyship speaks to the individual, it seems only apropos that starting from a place of centering oneself (in the context of critical reflection and self-awareness) is very necessary.

Where the focus is on the individual or the group, allies are expected to not only acknowledge, but to raise awareness of the social-communal and workplace inequities between people as a way to help make tangible these negative tropes and trends and their harmful or unfair consequences and impacts.

In a social setting, allyship could manifest itself as challenging a peer's antiquated terminology or exclusive/insensitive language. In the workplace, this could be demonstrated by supporting or sponsoring the ideas or events of a marginalized person or group. Some of examples of this could include sponsoring an LGBTQ affiliated student organization's event or providing support to one or more of your Black or Latina/o employees efforts to embark on a new venture that they otherwise might be not be able to.

68

A DIAMOND IS A DIAMOND

Due to its roots in outreach and verbal empowerment, allyship, is viewed by many as a tier-1 approach to social justice when compared to advocacy. Where allyship is to the individual(s) and advocacy is to the cause. Demonstrating one's commitment to allyship is oftentimes demands less physical action than advocacy. For example, where an advocate may join a peaceful protest, an ally might verbally shut down a discriminatory comment.

This perception of allyship is what results in the practice being positioned as rhetorical support in the work of social justice. This is not to say the work of an ally is to be dismissed, in fact, it is quite the contrary. The allied approach is one that is important and integral to the work of social justice.

Understanding one's capacity for change and how much one is able (or willing) to offer to the struggle ultimately determines the effectiveness of a person's efforts. It is essential to remember that both allyship and advocacy are a journey and we need to be mindful to not over extend ourselves in moments that call for a level of engagement beyond our readiness at that time. In figure 2, I will provide examples of how allyship connotes closely to rhetorical support.

Allyship = Rhetorical Support

Suggestive	Allies need only to speak up on behalf of other identities (generally those most marginalized) as a way of demonstrating support. For example, this could be the person serving on the Gender Inclusive Housing committee who suggests the team incorporate the perspective of the Director of the LGBTQ Center when making final decisions.
Credibility	One does not necessarily have to prove one is an ally nor should attempting to or focusing on proving one's allyship be at the center of one's ally practice and behavior. A minimum requisite for considering and calling oneself an ally calls for individuals or groups to simply state (when appropriate) that they have used their caché or influence to act in the interest of another (often marginalized) identity.

	Allyship oftentimes is not demonstrable.
Micro-Awareness	The mind of an ally is closely tied to micro-awareness as the focus tends to be on a singular event or circumstance. This person might view the matter(s) directly in front of them with great intentionality and seek to make a change, even if only temporary.
Safer	Although speaking up can bring very serious (undue) consequences to an ally, when compared to advocacy, allyship is viewed as the safer option as it requires little to no demonstration outside of verbal affirmation. It can be done in theory by adhering to the ideals of allyship, or in practice by speaking up and out on behalf of another.

Figure 2

Notwithstanding, all forms of allyship signify a clear commitment to social justice and require a sense of vulnerability and exposure. This willingness to be open can be categorized into three stages, typically resulting in low-risk, mid-risk, or high-risk allyship behavior.

Low-risk allyship is allyship that requires the least amount of vulnerability while still entailing a sense of exposure. Allies who engage in low-risk allyship are not looking to make a name as a large-scale change-agent, but rather, are looking to give a voice to the voiceless in that particular moment. This person might not always take this position, but they will feel comfortable challenging certain situations from time to time. Mid-risk allyship is allyhsip that requires a greater amount of vulnerability and a comfortability with engaging discomfort.

Allies who engage in mid-risk allyship are intentional about addressing the differences in the ways people are treated but do so in ways that do not jeopardize their positionality/career and still support their positive reputation. Finally, high-risk allyship is allyhsip that requires the greatest amount of vulnerability and a propensity to bring attention to injustices and inequities internally and externally. Allies who engage in high-risk allyship are inclined to use their privilege as a vehicle to represent and defend marginalized groups and individuals, even at the expense of their own reputation or privileged status. See Figure 2-A for examples of each level of risk regarding allyship.

A DIAMOND IS A DIAMOND

Levels of Risk: Allyship

High-Risk	High-Risk allyship might be portrayed as a person who attends a controversial public demonstration with high media and police presence and, thus, high visibility and exposure to a larger audience.
Mid-Risk	Mid-Risk allyship might be portrayed as a person who openly acknowledges that the positive reinforcement given to the White candidate was not afforded to the candidate of color.
Low-Risk	Low-Risk allyship might be portrayed as a person hearing an inappropriate joke or comment in a private or social setting and intervening.

Figure 2-A

Advocacy

The Pennsylvania State University defines advocacy as "Organized efforts aimed at influencing public attitudes, policies, and laws to create a more socially just society guided by the vision of human rights that may include awareness of socio-economic inequities, protection of social rights as well as racial identity, experiences of oppression, and spirituality (www.equity.psu.edu). The biggest difference between Penn State's definition of advocacy and Suffolk University's definition of allyship is that advocacy calls for a level of demonstrable action that is not expected of allyship in the same way.

Advocacy is also reflective of one's macro-awareness where allyship would harken more closely to one's micro-awareness of the matter. Where the focus is on the cause, macro-aware advocates are expected to challenge the larger systems of oppression and discrimination with intentionality.

In social movements, this could manifest as joining a march for equity, or exercising your first amendment right to a peaceful protest not just on behalf of a person or people, but on behalf of the larger cause. Whereas in the workplace, advocacy could be demonstrated by actively pursuing ways to challenge exclusive norms and traditions or by providing opportunities of success to marginalized employees through promotion, raises, chairwo/manship opportunities, or other leadership possibilities. See Figure 3 for how advocacy connotes demonstrable action.

A DIAMOND IS A DIAMOND

Advocacy = Demonstrable Action

Bystander Effect	When one's own identities are not being challenged or oppressed, one has the choice to opt into what I call the "bystander effect;" the decision to turn away from advocating on behalf of the targeted identity.
Macro-Awareness	The mind of an advocate is closely tied to macro-awareness as the focus tends to be on the larger, often systemic undercurrent that drives a particular call to action. This person might recognize an inequity and seek to find a more permanent solution to the issue that ultimately results in systemic disruption
Morality Check	A failed attempt or missed opportunity to advocate on behalf of oppressed identities tends to weigh heavily on social justice advocates.
Security Threat	The beauty of social justice can also be found in the irony, that is *social justice*

	inherently acknowledges social injustice. Advocacy is an inherent commitment to upsetting the established order, which is the essence of social justice.

Figure 3

Like allyship, advocacy also manifests as high-risk, mid-risk, and low-risk. Low-risk advocacy is advocacy that requires the least amount of activity while still requiring a strong level of engagement. Advocates who engage in low-risk advocacy are not looking to induce a level of exposure that attracts the media, but rather, are looking to raise awareness in a significant way that garners the attention of the people most closely related to the issue. Mid-risk advocacy is advocacy that requires a much greater amount of activity and, at times, a willingness to account for one's actions at a higher level.

Advocates who engage in mid-risk advocacy are comfortable with using their status, resources, and bodies to activate change in a locale or society. Though the impact is great and has strong potential for long-term change, mid-risk advocates generally operate on a timeline and will only engage in this this level of advocacy until their own needs and necessities become questioned. Finally, high-risk advocacy is advocacy that demands the greatest amount of activity and a willingness to put oneself in harm's way, physically, mentally, emotionally, spiritually, positionally, or financially. Advocates who engage in high-risk

76

advocacy are inclined to use their privilege, status, skills, resources, and power as a vehicle to exact change regardless of the consequence. Although high-risk advocacy is typically very well thought-out and far from reckless, one's moral view of the circumstance is valued to a greater degree than the possible negative outcomes of the decision. High-risk advocacy almost always effects long term change at either the local level or greater. See Figure 3-A for examples of each level of risk regarding advocacy.

Levels of Risk: Advocacy

High-Risk	High-risk advocacy might be where one uses their authority to pass a controversial executive order or make a grand change in workplace policy, especially against the will of others. in order to rectify a history of marginalization or oppression as a way to benefit marginalized people. It might also be the leader of a social justice movement who organizes people in vast numbers to interrupt the daily activities of others in order to call awareness to issues that have long been ignored.

Mid-Risk	Mid-risk advocacy might be walking out, striking, or boycotting an organization, corporation, or otherwise entity as a way to show resistance to the discriminatory or oppressive positionality of that entity.
Low-Risk	Low-risk advocacy might be crafting a petition in support of a social justice issue that has the potential to reach a vast number of people.

Figure 3-A

Finding Your Niche

In our Visceral Change workshop, *Effective Radicals: An Approach to Social Change from Baldwin to Davis*, the legendary Dr. Stephanie T. Robbins and I talk about the notion of "finding your niche." This is important because, if we accept allyship as the first tier of what understanding social justice looks like in practice, then the challenge with transitioning into advocacy from allyship is the fear the outcome. People tend to fear certain levels of conflict and more than that, consequence, which makes allyship, at first face, seem much more appealing. This is because advocacy, as we know, can generally carry higher levels of weight.

However, in either situation, each of us engage in what I call a "cost/benefit analysis" before we ever decide to become an ally or advocate for the likes and rights of ourselves or others. For women and people of color, for example, there is a very real risk of being reprimanded unjustly if they decide to advocate for themselves in unjust or inequitable situations, especially if it's done with fervor, as there is the reinforced stigma of being the "angry black woman" or being labeled incompetent.

Each of these, and many more, serve as cause for apprehension for people who are well intentioned allies striving to be advocates. A piece of this apprehension, too, is due to the fact that most people tend to believe that real change can only spawn from a radical approach to social justice and that a more conservative approach might be in vain. However, in reality, one's niche can be radical while not mirroring the work of, say, Malcolm X or Dr. Angela Davis. What's more, the interesting about the word "radical" is that it is often coupled with a negative connotation. We tend to view those who act radically as either extreme in their beliefs, disruptive beyond reproach, or even supporters of harm.

For example, if I were to challenge one to think about the radical figures of the Civil Rights Movement, it stands to reason that one would immediately consider the likes of Malcolm X or Angela Davis—and rightfully so, as both of them were unquestionably outspoken and radical in the ways they challenged the system(s) of oppression at that time. Each called attention, unapologetically, to severe racial injustice, centuries in the making, that had been willfully ignored for far too long. Each were instrumental in establishing counter narratives and through and within communities of color that intended to upend and confront White doctrines and racist ideologies: Malcolm X, did this via the Nation of Islam and Dr. Angela Davis did this through participation in the Black Panther Party. Both were considered so threatening to the White agenda, that their work was impeded by government intervention – Malcolm X being wire tapped and murdered, and Angela Davis being placed on the FBI's Most Wanted List. Years later the Reagan administration would attempt to remove her tenure as a professor at the University of California, Berkeley.

In the recollection of Civil Rights Era radicals, less likely to come to mind (or at least with less immediacy) would be Lorraine Hansberry or James Baldwin. However, they were just as radical as Malcolm X and Angela Davis. Why is this the case? The answer is simple – Baldwin and Hansberry radically challenged the system using different methods and measures. Their radical activities manifested not in the form of organizing and leading protests and marches—though they did take participatory roles in those contexts, but rather, their preferred tools were writing, speaking, literary arts and storytelling.

A DIAMOND IS A DIAMOND

Baldwin, a literary genius and Hansberry, a brilliant playwright, exposed the woeful nature of what it meant to be a Negro in America in ways that attracted hopeful White allies to the struggle. The artistic, politically-driven, literary forms they created allowed them to find favor with White elites. This granted them access to spaces wherein they were able to share their work to reach and influence diverse audiences. Ultimately, Hansberry and Baldwin even gained access to the White House, for a meeting with (then) Attorney General, Robert F. Kennedy, to discuss the racial desegregation of US schools and the accompanying challenges of Black life in America and the experiences of racism and inequality of which they wrote.

Malcolm X, Dr. Angela Davis, Lorraine Hansberry, and James Baldwin were all equally influential in the Civil Rights Movements of the 50s, 60s and 70s. And they were all radical truth-tellers in their own right and indifferent parts of the same conversation about racism, capitalism and injustice. However, what makes each of their individual advocacy most effective, potent and unique was their ability to have identified the niche that best allowed them to capitalize on their existing strengths, talents, interests and experiences. The same principle applies to all aspiring social justice advocates, especially those who feel powerless in their positions, whatever they may be.

It is important to remember that, although the transition from allyship to advocacy can be challenging and at times risky, it is absolutely possible once you can identify and begin working through and within your niche. For some, that may be writing a strongly worded letter to the President, Dean, or Director clearly outlining and articulating the inequities a marginalized or vulnerable group has encountered; while for others, the niche may be empowering others to be the change they want to see by intentionally appointing specific people to positions of power in order to shift inequitable dynamics from within.

As you develop during your journey, be sure to ask yourself, "What's my niche?" And equally important: remember that allies and advocates follow the lead of the marginalized or oppressed group(s) that they seek to support. Allies and advocates support and act *in the service of* non-dominant or less powerful individuals, groups and communities.

In Closing

It is my belief that the Core Five Components outlined and overviewed in this guidebook, are necessary for understanding social justice and developing critical consciousness. Through power and privilege, we learn how there are things in this world that we need not concern ourselves with should we not want to specifically due to our privileged positions in society. Identity and intersectionality teaches us how it is the relationship to the privileges our social identities, and those intersecting, receive that cause us to behave in problematic and discriminatory ways. The third component, systems of socialization, teaches us how internal and external influences play a major role in conditioning us to believe the ideologies that ultimately govern our discriminatory and oppressive points of view. Finally, it is through an understanding of cultural competency that we begin to reexamine how we orient ourselves towards individuals and groups in hopes of better understanding our differences en route to evoking a level of acceptance and support among all communities.

As we transition into allyship and advocacy on our journey towards justice, I remind my readers once more of how the beauty of social justice also lies in its irony; that *social justice inherently acknowledges social injustice*. Were this untrue, then individuals and organizations would not require social justice or diversity training.

Part of the initial challenge of engaging in social justice work with institutions and organizations involves the fact that by calling for this work, the leadership of that space is acknowledging the presence of inequity and lack of diversity and inclusion which is likely accompanied by racism, bias, homophobia, sexism or anti-LGBTQ sentiment.

In my experience, there aren't many people in high-level leadership positions who are willing to acknowledge these disparities and inequities. In addition to acknowledgement, leadership must then be willing to allocate the necessary time, labor and material resources required for socially just institutional transformation driven and sustained by a commitment to diversity, equity and inclusion.

The Core Five Components to Social Justice is intended to serve as a foundational set of tools that we can use to get ourselves to a space where we become gradually able to *disassociate in order to dismantle*. In other words, we want to **disassociate** ourselves from the internalization and perpetuation of privileges that are coupled with our identities (as determined and conferred by unfair systems) as a way to **dismantle** these systems and structures that govern our society. If we can do that, then we will have initiated our journey into consciousness and understanding of identity in relation to diversity, equity and inclusion en route to creating a more socially just world.

PART 2

WORKPLACE
APPLICATION

Part 2: Workplace Application

In Part 2 of this book, I will provide some brief but concrete takeaways and recommendations that will help you begin to apply these five concepts in workplace environments. To help guide your understanding, my recommendations and takeaways will be divided into two categories: Employee Support and Policy and Procedural Changes. This section should be of specific interest to employees of any particular organization or institution who are actively seeking ways to engage diversity, inclusion, equity, and social justice in the workplace.

A fundamental part of the work of Multicultural Organizational Development and Inclusive Excellence is the call for a systemic approach to diversity and inclusion. Traditionally, initiatives of equity in the workplace have manifested as either one-off training and development workshops, or the formation of a diversity committee. However, true long-term results of diversity, inclusion, and equity in the workplace can only become apparent through systemic intervention.

WORKPLACE APPLICATION

POWER & PRIVILEGE

Core Five Component 1: Power & Privilege

Using one's access to power and privilege is critical when instituting changes in any organization. I am a firm believer that because most organizations operate through hierarchy, real change begins at the top; it is disproportionately true that the employees at the top (CEOs, Presidents, Executive Directors, Provosts, Deans, etc.) have more power & privilege to enact change than any other organizational member—except, perhaps, the whistle-blower…but I digress.

The problem, however, is that a vast majority of these high-profile stakeholders see their positions as that of "gatekeeper." That is, they use their platform as a way to keep things the way they are rather than rock the proverbial boat. What this does, of course, is create an incessant promulgation of elitist behaviors designed only to further oppress the individuals who lack the same levels of access and opportunities as those ultimately benefitting from the status quo. Thus, the fact that individuals with the aforementioned access enjoy such large influence in the outcomes experienced by you and I, is why I say that access to power and privilege are critical when instituting organizational change. Here's how:

Employee Support

In order to best serve your employees using power and privilege, you must first understand your own positionality in relation to these concepts. Your access to power and privilege will determine the ways in which you can actively

challenge systems to support your employees at all levels—
staff, faculty, coworkers and peers. A diverse unit is going
to have a panoply of different experiences as well as
challenges that directly reflect the various identities
present. This means that it is imperative that organizational
leadership establish practices that honor the differing
degrees of support required by each identity group. For
example, I harken back to one of my core Visceral Change
principles – that is - *"we all struggle equally, but our
struggles are not the same."*

In sum, this statement declares that there are certain
experiences that, on average and by and large, most people
could argue are commonplace. A few examples of this
would be enduring a difficult break up or struggling
financially. However, we need know, too, that one cannot
treat the Black struggle the same way one would treat the
Native or Indigenous struggle. One cannot treat the QLGB
(queer, lesbian, gay, bisexual) struggle the same way one
would treat the Transgender struggle. This is because,
despite how common our experiences with struggle are, the
truth is that our identities and positionalities cause our
struggles to differ…not necessarily emotionally but more
so politically and socially. If we fail to take these identities
into account in relation to our struggles, we end up
promulgating identity blindness, which only leads to false
equivalencies and the invalidation of distinct experiences.

It is imperative that organizations provide the necessary
space and support for their employees at all times,
regardless of identity, but it's equally important to keep

identities in mind when addressing some concerns. I think about my own experience as a Black employee working in Higher Education. I remember being employed at a Predominantly White Institution during the same time that the murders of Philando Castille and Alton Sterling occurred. At that time, these murders were the most recent episodes in what seemed like a decade (or even centuries) long, fractured relationship between the Black community and law enforcement.

For many people who were not Black, this was just another high profile event in the unfortunate cycle of police violence against Blacks, but for me this was the continuation of the theme Black life as disposable. It was yet another example of the ways in which racism manifests in the United States. Thus, immediately following the murders of Philando Castille and Alton Sterling, it was important that I take a day off to focus on myself and my own healing and wellbeing. Fortunately, I had a supervisor, a White man, who possessed a level of racial literacy and cultural competence that compelled him to not only ask me how I was doing, but to offer up any resources he could provide, including giving me some time off (personal leave) if necessary.

In the days following the murders he called a leadership meeting specifically to dialogue around the recent social issues, with a focus on how we might better serve and assist our campus community. My supervisor demonstrated how to use one's power and privilege, both professionally and personally, as a means of advocacy for marginalized

90

identities and to improve the overall community. His access to agency allowed him to leverage his Whiteness to prioritize diversity and social justice in ways that propelled our work to the forefront of inclusive excellence.

Policy & Procedural Changes

When using power and privilege to address policies and procedures, it's important to remember the type of access each change agent has afforded to them. It is my belief that the most immediate and longest-lasting organizational change stems from the leadership level. Presidents, HR Heads, Provosts, Executive Directors, Project Leaders, and positions of the like, all have the capacity to institute ripple-like change that spreads downward, upward, and outward. Oftentimes, however, what ends up happening is that the leadership level is composed mostly of the folks who are benefitting from the current state of affairs in terms of policies and procedures.

Some individuals in leadership might also hail from marginalized identity groups and still refuse to see the challenges or inadequacies present in current policy—one of the more important demonstrations of the impact and importance of intersectionality. What I mean by this is that if a White woman ascends to an executive position mainly held by men, she may think that all women can follow in her path, failing to recognize that policy barriers still exist for women of color, women with disabilities, and queer women. In this case, intersectionality helps us to see that women's experiences are mediated by gender and sexuality, race and ethnicity, and disability status.

If you are reading this as a member of your organization's leadership team, then it is incumbent upon you to identify ways to utilize the agency associated with your privilege in order to make change. According to Visceral Change, it takes approximately five-years to affect large-scale cultural shifts in most institutions. That means with concerted effort, the organization we see today is guaranteed to look, feel, and operate entirely differently five-years from now.

The first step in intentionally shifting an organizational culture is to revisit the policies and procedures that already exist. For example, on college campuses, some buildings such as residence halls do not allow open flames in or outside of their premises as it is a clear fire hazard. The one exception for many institutions is with regard to social events that involve grilling, like a bbq or a pot luck.

However, this policy does not benefit Native American students who practice the burning of cedar and sage for traditional purposes. The University of North Dakota has developed a verifiable cedar and sage policy that allows for the burning of materials inside of a controlled container or object (www.und.edu), as well as other potential necessities that honor and value the cultural heritage and practices of underserved or underrepresented group needs or causes.

A DIAMOND IS A DIAMOND

We at Visceral Change recommend that all organizations, from large scale departments to lower-tier offices and units, revisit their policies and procedures every three to five years, minimally. This allows you to not only be in direct accordance with the time it takes to shift an organizational culture, but it also allows you to remain current with the needs of your population. Committees, at the behest of the executive leadership, should be formed or duties should be assigned where the principal focus is to revisit policies and procedures that exceed the five-year mark.

Leadership needs to take the lead here to model the significance of addressing policy and as a measure of accountability. Far too often, it's the people at the highest level who think the least about the challenges and misfortune of others. By centering positive or progressive uses of power and privilege in your organizational change efforts, Leadership begins to send a message to their staff that they understand the importance of inclusive excellence, if not social justice.

WORKPLACE APPLICATION

IDENTITY & INTERSECTIONALITY

A DIAMOND IS A DIAMOND

Core Five Component 2: Identity & Intersectionality

Understanding the ways in which identity and intersectionality operate in the workplace is crucial to understanding how to best create an inclusive environment. The challenges (and frankly the dangers) of homogenous representation at the leadership level are timeless representations of how systems work to maintain the margins and the identities that reside there. It is still especially rare to see people of color in leadership positions.

In all the years of the United States, there has only been one Black President and no women or openly LGBTQ-identified person to occupy the post. Homogenous units in institutions and organizations are evidentiary of the ways in which people of color, in particular, continue to be ostracized from the benefits of professional success. Much of the time, the challenges faced by employees have a lot to do with the lack of representation or advocacy from a supervisor or overall leadership that either looks like them or identifies similarly. Like privilege, owning a keen understanding of the ways in which one's identities can impact the workplace is critical to shaping your organization's culture.

Employee Support

Employing a staff with diverse identities should be the goal for all departments and organizations. Diversity, as we know, is the cornerstone of brave ideas, robust cultural expression, and sustainable environments. Diverse staffs provide fresh and true avenues of thought comprised of variegated points of view, experiences, and perspectives: but like I say in my workshop on diversifying your hiring, "When you hire diverse people, you take on diverse issues." In supporting employees from diverse backgrounds, it's important to consider the many challenges that come with them.

For a lot of people hailing from diverse backgrounds, many have had to negotiate the nuances of their identities when considering their workplace comportment. For example, a Black woman who has endured microaggressive behaviors one time too many, and finally feels compelled to express her anger and frustration surrounding the incident has to bear the burden of considering the social consequences of her mode of expression in addressing the situation.

The threat of being labeled in accordance with the "angry Black woman" stereotype serves as more than a mere pejorative – it becomes a career defining characteristic, albeit a profoundly unfair one. Thus, Black women are forced to harbor and internalize justifiable feelings of anger and frustration, ultimately leading to the development of unhealthy stress and possible damage to their career longevity.

A DIAMOND IS A DIAMOND

Though the above example featured Black women, the scenario described tends to hold true for virtually all people of color. Black men and Latina women are often hyper-sexualized, to the point where Title IX claims and stigmas predicated upon assumptions of promiscuity need little to no proof of validation. In keeping with racist stereotypes, Native and Indigenous Peoples tend to be thought of as inept and unintelligent by virtue of their strong cultural and heritage traditions and commitments.

These often unfounded and largely unfair preconceptions have much to do with the ways in which people of color operate within a system that was not designed for their success. Thus, it becomes incumbent upon employers, especially those with the access to power and privilege, to challenge these false notions and identity-based biases by finding ways to support the achievements and successes of marginalized peoples.

Melody Hobson, the Fortune 500 CEO of Ariel Investments, said in her Ted Talk – *Color Blind or Color Brave*, that a hiring chair once asked whether he was expected to hire the best candidate or the diverse candidate, to which the response he received was "yes." What employers can do is begin promoting marginalized people into positions that challenge these long-standing stigmas. Leadership has the power to foreground initiatives and support assignments championed by individuals who possess these identities. In so doing, leaders have an opportunity to model the values and priorities of institutional commitment to diversity and inclusion. A

97

socially just approach to supervision requires an understanding of identity - and the organization that is able to recognize the beauty and richness in their staff's diversity will be successful in cultivating and retaining multicultural talent.

Policy & Procedural Changes

Adequately shifting one's organizational culture has to first begin with revisiting and ultimately reframing the organization's current policies and procedures. There is an old adage we use at Visceral Change to encourage effective change in organizational development: *adapt the market to the message, not the message to the market.* This means that organizations should commit to holistic transformation in order to make change.

By adapting the market to the message, you are recognizing that what you are currently practicing is not or has not been working. You are demonstrating that you are willing to change your company's direction in order to accomplish your ultimate goal of diversity and inclusion as central to your organizational development.

The challenge for most units is that they are unwilling to accept that what they have been doing is either not working or cannot be made to work for the employees they serve. Thus, instead of adapting their market to the message, they adapt the message to the market. This means that they identify areas of the message that work for their overall interests and apply them at their leisure and discretion.

98

A DIAMOND IS A DIAMOND

What this ultimately leads to is an organization that operates on extremes – heavily favoring some people or identities while consciously or unconsciously marginalizing others. The messaging in your policy and procedural changes has to be consistent and built around intersectionality.

Consider the tenure and promotion process used by colleges and universities. This process varies among different institutional types, according to legacy, prestige and other aspects of institutional designation. For the most part, regardless of institutional type, faculty candidates are evaluated along three required domains: teaching, research and service. For some candidates, this means publishing 2 books and for others it means publishing 10 articles in top-ranked, peer-reviewed journals.

At Research 1 institutions, however, a much greater emphasis is given to the research requirement of tenure and promotion than, say, service. At prima facie, this would make sense given that the word "research" is applied to the institutional classification. However, the problem is that most of the departments operating within these institutional types give little to no credence to service at all, which is where most academicians of color find themselves dedicating a majority or substantial portion of their time. In an article published by Karen Kelsky in the Chronicle of Higher Education, she states:

> At many research-oriented
> institutions, for example, it will be
> something like 40 percent research, 30
> percent teaching, and 30 percent
> service. At the very top research
> powerhouse universities, it may be 60
> research/30 teaching/10 service.
> (Kelsky, K. 2017)

It can take anywhere from 6-9 years on average to receive tenure depending on the institution. For professors of color at Research 1 institutions, though, they can easily average around the top end of this range simply because of the amount of service they provide to their students, communities of color and institutional committee work.

This also means that many professors of color (rare in elite and Research 1 settings) often struggle when it comes to tenure and promotion because they have to negotiate whether or not they are willing to tell students of color that they cannot commit to mentoring them. These scholars are also faced with the very real possibility that if they say no to serving on department and college-level committees, there will be *no person of color* on said committee.

Where service is not considered to be an area of importance that is held in the same regard as teaching or research, it inherently disadvantages faculty of color who are constantly thinking about the students of color who receive less opportunities and support during their time in college. Further, the devaluation of service elides the creation of diverse committee membership, which directly impacts many facets of institutional decision-making and function. The policies for tenure and promotion, as they stand, are challenging for faculty of color at many institutions. A quick and easy adjustment university departments can make would involve repositioning or elevating service to a higher status for consideration when evaluating performance for tenure and promotion.

This would allow faculty, specifically faculty of color and transgender faculty, to confidently and comfortably support their students and engage in institutional diversity work in the ways that align with their personal and professional code of ethics, while also focusing on their research and teaching.

WORKPLACE APPLICATION

SYSTEMS OF SOCIALIZATION

A DIAMOND IS A DIAMOND

Core Five Component 3: Systems of Socialization

The obvious question posed by most readers might be: *how does one incorporate systems of socialization into shifting organizational culture?* In response, I implore my skeptics to remember that by 'socialization,' I mean 'conditioning.' In other words, I am referring to the ways in which we, as employees and as people, are indoctrinated into society's standards for what is considered as 'normal.' Often justified as "traditional practice," socialization has always influenced or directly informed the organizational systems and policies to which institutions adhere. Below are some strategies and areas of consideration when contemplating systems of socialization for your organizational shifts.

Employee Support

Many employees owning marginalized identities already face subjugation on their first day of employment. The unjust social stigmas and preconceived notions that come with being an Asian transracial adoptee or a Punjabi Sikh oftentimes set the tone for the rest of one's career in their particular place of employment. As a peer, colleague, or supervisor of a person with marginalized identities, it becomes important that you remain highly attuned to the social stigmas surrounding said identities. This tends to play a most vital role when considering the ways in which the lack of opportunities and access adversely affect employee performance or potential for promotion.

Supporting one's employees has just as much to do with remaining conscious about the social order as it does with ensuring that folks feel safe in their identities at work. Many employers (especially in the professional sector) operate in predominantly White agencies and organizations whose traditions and values generally support those of similar backgrounds and identities. One of the biggest challenges employees with marginalized identities face is finding community within a space that was and is not structurally designed for their comfort or success.

In my presentation titled, *"All Aboard!: Diversifying Your Hiring with All Intents and Purposes,"* I talk about the different challenges organizations face when attempting to diversify their hiring, as well as the struggles employees face when hired into homogenous environments. One of my takeaways comes in the form of a reminder I share with people of color, which is this: "sometimes in order to bring the diversity you have to **be** the diversity." In other words, in order to recruit and engage other diverse candidates in hopes of them joining you in struggle and success at your current place of employment, it behooves you, at times, to be as involved in the hiring process as possible.

Diverse candidates want to relate to other diverse candidates and know that support can be found in an individual if not an institution. They want someone who will be real with them about the culture of the place and even about practical concerns about the neighborhood and demographic surrounding the place of employment. Of course, a diverse candidate can do research to find statistics online, but they want to hear about the day to day living experience that someone who looks like them has in that community.

However, I also talk about the taxation this (ideally) voluntary undertaking of "being the diversity to bring more diversity" places on the marginalized employee. The reality of constantly applying oneself as the diversity champion simply to bring other diverse candidates can feel exploitative and also exhausting for the employee. This is why organizations who are working towards diversity need to remain in touch with the social climate. This will help them understand the challenging optics and material realities of allowing their one or two employees with marginalized identities continue to perform the unpaid (and often emotional) labor associated with diversifying their staff.

An understanding of societal/social contexts allows the employer to recognize how these employees are tasked with this burden even outside of the workplace and are quietly (not by choice, but for job security) hoping that their colleagues and supervisors of dominant identities will step up and lead the charge for diverse and inclusive change. A shift in this dynamic also means a shift in retention for your marginalized employees.

One way that organizations can use their understanding of social systems to support one's staff is to consider developing Affinity Groups. These are working groups or communal spaces for employees to share with one another based on a common identity or salient, mutual interest. For example, while working at most of my previous institutions, I noticed very quickly that the environment was very White, male, and heteronormative, among other things. In order to support the people who felt most marginalized, I created Affinity Groups as a way to bring non-dominant identities together in an effort to find community. Examples of these Affinity Group are: *Staff of Color Affinity Group, LGBTQ in Student Affairs Affinity Group, Gamers and Techies Affinity Group*, and *Women in Leadership Affinity Group*, to name a few.

These groups served as safe spaces on campus for members to congregate and discuss the challenges and joys of being who they are, where they are and to support one another. Some Affinity Groups have even developed concrete action plans to specifically address the inequities they see developing in the workplace. Most importantly, Affinity Groups have proven to be powerful retention tools, serving as the impetus for a staff or faculty member's decision to remain in their particular department or unit, since they have been able to find community despite their marginalized status within the larger employee population.

Policy & Procedural Changes

Optically, the policies and procedures of a given organization or department should also be clear about the ways in which they represent their staff. For example, over the past few years, a particular university in the Southwestern United States has undergone an institution-wide organizational development process that saw turnover and attrition at all levels of the university. From the installation of a new university president to the departures of entry-level employees, the reorganizing of the university looked more like an active practice in racism and sexism than it did a strengths-based organizational restructuring.

In 2018, one particular department came under severe scrutiny for their handling of the removal of two Black male employees. The department used their organizational development process (within the context of the larger institutional restructuring), which saw most of their higher-level positions being staffed with White women (and one White man) as an opportunity to rebrand.

Part of this new branding negatively reimagined the optics of leadership resulting in the removal of the aforementioned Black employees, both of whom were operating successfully at the Leadership level. Their contracts were "non-renewed" for reasons unknown. When one of the Black male employees inquired as to why he was being released from employment, he was told that "no appointed professionals are guaranteed another contract" regardless of high quality job performance.

Although problematic for obvious reasons, the statement made by the Executive Director emanated from a university policy. Unfortunately, it was true that the institutional contract for professional staff classified them as 'at will employees' whose employment may be terminated at any time for any reason that does not violate public law. Both employees, each of them Directors – were let go without reasonable justification other than because the policies of the university, in conjunction with racist sentiments, made it possible.

The most important danger to consider with this type of policy is that any individual in a position of power, such as that of an Executive Director or Dean of Students, can exercise a racist or homophobic or otherwise bias-oriented agenda and be completely protected by the language of the policy while doing so. This practice of 'at will employees' and appointed professional contracts is commonly used nationwide; one institutional example can be found here - (www.hr.arizona.edu). Such policies should be re-written to ensure that the rights of the employee are not violated, and that due process is followed in human resource decisions involving employee demotion, suspension or termination.

Another relevant notation is that, amidst the height of the **#MeToo** and **#TimesUp** movements, the same American Southwestern university mentioned above saw two lawsuits that involved three women Deans and a woman of color Executive Director, each of whom sued on the grounds of racial and gender discrimination. The lawsuit resulted in the university being ordered by the court to pay over one-million dollars to the plaintiffs. A separate lawsuit was brought against the university (and settled out of court) over the removal of their highest-ranking Diversity Officer (a Hispanic man) due to the mismanagement of that process, as well.

A DIAMOND IS A DIAMOND

The university's lack of social conditions and societal awareness caused them to continue to operate in a manner that was antiquated and inconsistent with contemporary issues regarding race and gender equity. Because the university eschewed or ignored social movements for race and gender justice (and the changes these movements spawned) it missed the opportunity to adjust and to correct the damages done by the discriminatory policies that were in place and weaponized against marginalized employees. Their adherence to and perpetuation of the social stigmas that have oppressed women and people of color for centuries carried over to their handling of misconduct and discrimination at the university level.

Thus, it becomes ever so important for organizations to ensure that their policies and procedures adhere to Equal Employment Opportunity standards and remain current with respect to the various identities of the world, especially for those who are marginalized. Institutions and organizations have the ability to reframe their practices by centering social justice in all that they do.

WORKPLACE APPLICATION

CULTURAL COMPETENCE

Core Five Component 4: Cultural Competence

I mentioned this in passing above, but I reiterate it now because the statement itself holds a great deal of relevance here: it takes five-years of sustained effort to create a large-scale cultural shift within an institution or organization. A part of this has to do with the training and onboarding of new and existing professionals, but the bulk of this timeline speaks to ever-changing social concerns cultural issues that either adversely or favorably impact one's staff or workforce.

A prime example of this is the 2016 election of Donald Trump as United States President. This election, for many White Americans, served as a historic moment in our country's existence where the state of the Union would venture back to the "glory days" of yesteryear; but glorious for whom? For many marginalized identities such as people of color and LGBTQ folks, specifically those of Chicano, Middle-Eastern and Hispanic descent, Trump's election signified a momentous move backward, propelling the nation into a divisive regression, activating hate groups such as the "Alt-Right" and the "White Nationalist Movement."

This national event impacted many organizations and institutions around the country, causing hiring practices to heavily favor homogeneity and Right-Wing pundits to infiltrate and blatantly spout hatred on college campuses under the guise of Free Speech and the protections afforded by the First Amendment. In remaining current with these cultural trends, institutions and organizations stand a better chance of keeping inclusivity at the center of their praxis in order to provide a more encouraging and overall safer environment for their employees.

Employee Support

In a time of cultural shift, it is important for organizations to support their employees in as many ways as possible. With the country being as polarized as it is and the government placing the pressure on one's rights to free speech, organizations must have support systems in place for their employees who may find themselves impacted at a greater rate than others.

A November 2017 Washington Post article reported that in 2016, the United States saw a rise in hate crimes with more than 300 reports targeting Muslim identified people (www.washingtonpost.com). That same year and month, an LA Times article published a story exposing the inequities and mismanagement of American citizens by ICE and other American government affiliates. The article found that:

> Since 2002, Immigration and Customs Enforcement has wrongly identified at least 2,840 United States citizens as possibly eligible for deportation, and at least 214 of them were taken into custody for some period of time, according to ICE records analyzed by the Transactional Records Access

Clearinghouse at Syracuse University. (www.latimes.com)

For many of our employees, colleagues, peers, and supervisors, the aforementioned cases serve as a reminder of everyday life. Personally, as a Black man, there are many life skills I practice before, during, and after work, in order to ensure a level of safety and security for myself and those I am responsible for. Like me, individuals who relate to the statistics above spend much of their day reconciling how to maneuver in and out of an environment that was not designed for their success nor for their safety.

As a result, it becomes incumbent upon leadership within organizations to cultivate environments that don't just support safe spaces for growth and development—but create and maintain programs and resources that empower their most marginalized employees to strive for success, at least within the context and space of the organization. Remaining attuned to the effects of cultural and climate shifts will allow your organization to position itself as a local, regional, and even national leader in inclusivity.

Employees not only want to work for an organization that values diversity and inclusion, they want to work someplace where they can see growth in opportunities over time, with safe identity spaces (in theory and practice) being visible and supported. As a Black man who is faced with inevitable challenges as a result of my intersecting identities in society, the workplace should be one space where I can find comfort and relief from what goes on

113

outside the walls. Our job as leaders in the workplace is to make sure we are doing all that we can to value our employees by paying attention and not contributing to the stigmas, stereotypes and negative trends that may be circulating in the greater society.

Policy & Procedural Changes

Harkening back to the First Amendment for a moment, this is a topic that has seen a rise in its popularity as an institutional buzzword in ways we have never previously encountered. It has become more and more imperative that institutions and organizations provide a clear set of standards and values for the areas of conduct they support and do not support.

In my work with institutions and organizations on the First Amendment, one common question I hear all the time is the obvious one: "What do we do?" After my workshops on this topic, a shared sentiment tends to shape the room, and that is: "So you're saying there is nothing we can really do to challenge White supremacy and overall hate speech?" My answer, of course, is No: we must all do our best to confront and dismantle White supremacy and hate speech and we have many tools for doing this work at our disposal. However, it needs to be made clear that the Constitution, especially the First Amendment, is one of the most difficult documents to articulate fairly because there is no singular interpretation of the language.

A DIAMOND IS A DIAMOND

Now this is not a book on legalities, though that is in the Visceral Change will likely tackle that area in the near future, but I do want to add some clarity if possible. On one hand, the decentralized approach to interpreting the Constitution can prove to be beneficial because it suggests that the document is alive and can be interpreted one way over the other to fit a variety of circumstances. On the other hand, the burden of proof is always on the state (or in this case, the offended) and thus, in order to discuss real change, one must first articulate how the language, in its current state and as it is presented, is offensive as is. That juxtaposition alone makes it difficult to challenge hate speech, as I explain in detail in my nationally recognized presentation, *Exhibit 14B: An Equal Rights Approach to the First Amendment.*

Regardless of one's feelings towards the way in which hate speech is addressed by the legal system and First Amendment scholars, I want everyone to know that there are a few actions you can deploy as an administration to expeditiously alleviate some of the tension:

1. **Restate your values as an institution/organization.** Often when institutions allow White nationalists and far right-wing pundits (like Richard Spencer and David Duke or Ben Shapiro and Tomi Loren) onto their campuses, the biggest administrative concern is that the institution supports the rhetoric of said speakers; this does not have to be true. If you're an institution or an organization that does not support the rhetoric

and/or positions of such speakers, the first thing your administration should do prior to, during, and after the speaker's visit is to restate your institutional/organizational values.

2. **Know your Free Speech Guidelines.** An understanding of the First Amendment plays an important role in addressing free speech issues in organizations or on college campuses (specifically public institutions). If your organization does not have a 1A Specialist or some equivalent, please consider either creating the position and hiring for one or compensating an existing employee (adequately) to take on these duties as an expansion of their workload/ job description. This will not only help your community feel safer and keep your employees more aligned with your organizational guidelines, but it will also set parameters for potential speakers whose intent is to share a problematic point of view.

3. **Encourage counter protesting.** In most cases, the pundits spewing hateful speech on college campuses are doing so under the guise of the First Amendment, so it is only right that we encourage others to evoke their First Amendment right to free speech and do the same. Any First Amendment scholar will tell you that the best way to battle speech is with more speech. Thus, make clear to your community that there are opportunities to counter protest should groups or individuals feel necessary and identify the designated areas on site.

WORKPLACE APPLICATION

ALLYSHIP & ADVOCACY

Core Five Component 5: Allyship & Advocacy

As I stated in the first half of this guidebook, Allyship and Advocacy speak to the utmost logical evolution of the Core Five: practice and action. The point in our journey where we take all that we have learned and begin to apply it. Whether in our personal, professional, social or academic lives, ally and advocate are two of the most important roles we can play as individuals.

There is no breakdown of employee support and policy and procedure changes in this section, because by now your understanding of the other four components should start to the light way. After all, the Core Five Components to Social Justice is designed to encourage growth in *you* and to implore you to find the courage to locate your voice and your niche, and to combine those aspects with your continued learning about the issues to persevere in your commitment to doing the work.

To support our peers through our allyship and advocacy is to use our privilege as a platform to support those who have less privilege. These occasions to act vary in degree and circumstance—but no feat of advocacy or allyship endeavor is too small. Whether it's overhearing sexist or Islamophobic language in the next cubical over or witnessing active bias at play in the hiring and selection process, it is important that you find your niche in advocacy in order to be most effective in whatever intervention you choose to make.

A DIAMOND IS A DIAMOND

In Closing

Not everyone is built to be the outspoken, public firebrand, type of advocate like Sojourner Truth or Fannie Lou Hamer. Some folks are built to advocate through arts and humanities like Richard Wright and Frida Kahlo. Others are called to do the work through and in the entertainment industry, like Spike Lee and Laverne Cox. While others are simply Chip Man!

Whatever the shape of your ally work or the scope of your niche in advocacy, know that your contributions to social justice work are necessary and important. There will always be cause to stand beside those whose voices are swallowed or silenced by oppressive systems and structures, so it is up to those of us who see "the arc of the universe bending toward justice," to make some noise.

In *A New Earth: Awakening to Your Life's Purpose*, Eckhart Tolle (2005) describes one's inner purpose as equivalent to one's state of 'being' which is primary; he describes one's outer purpose as one's state of 'doing' which is secondary. Tolle states that it is challenging to align one's outer purpose with one's inner purpose, but that the true fulfilment of one's life comes only when the two have met. (p. 258). In extrapolating from Tolle's point, I believe that as sentient beings complete with a soul, it is incumbent upon us to align our inner and outer purposes to transformed and accountable by and through our shared, ethical commitment to a more socially just world in all of the spaces and communities we occupy.

Reference List

Baldwin, J. (1965, March 7). The American Dream and the American Negro. Retrieved from http://movies2.nytimes.com/books/98/03/29/specials/baldw in-dream.html

Board, E. (2017, November 25). Hate in America is on the Rise. Retrieved from https://www.washingtonpost.com/opinions/hate-in-america-is-on-the-rise/2017

Crumpacker, Shapiro, & Vander Haegen. (n.d.). HIDDEN/UNCONSCIOUS BIAS: A PRIMER - Diversity - [PDF Document]. Retrieved from https://vdocuments.mx/hiddenunconscious-bias-a-primer-diversity.html

Employment Categories. (n.d.). Retrieved from https://hr.arizona.edu/supervisors/employment-benefits/employment-categories

Federal Bureau of Prisons. (n.d.). Retrieved from https://www.bop.gov/about/statistics/statistics_inmate_race .jsp

Fight on NYC 6 Train. (2012, April 02). Retrieved from https://youtu.be/Erlw-ODVZxU

Forbes-Vierling, S. (2017, October 14). Dark Skin Pain, Light Skin Privilege: Nine Solutions to Dismantling Colorism in the Black Community. Retrieved from https://medium.com/@suzanneforbesvierling/moving-forward-with-radical-action-nine-solutions-that-the-black-community-can-adopt-to-dismantle-8edfb15917cb

Highest Income Counties in 2011. (2012, September 20). Retrieved from https://www.washingtonpost.com/wp-srv/special/local/highest-income-counties/

Hook, J. N., Davis, D. E., Owen, J., Worthington, E. L., & Utsey, S. O. (2013). Cultural Humility Scale. PsycTESTS Dataset,353-366. doi:10.1037/t29547-000

Ingraham, C. (2017, December 06). The richest 1 percent now owns more of the country's wealth than at any time in the past 50 years. Retrieved from https://www.washingtonpost.com/news/wonk/wp/2017/12/06/the-richest-1-percent-now-owns-more-of-the-countrys-wealth-than-at-any-time-in-the-past-50-years/?noredirect=on&utm_term=.64d85017bd49

Johnson, Allan G. (2006) Privilege, Power and Difference. McGraw-Hill, New York.

(McIntosh, 1992; Robinson & Howard-Hamilton, 2000)

Johnson, M. (2016, December 5). Joe McKnight and the fear of the black man. Retrieved from https://theundefeated.com/features/joe-mcknight-and-the-fear-of-the-black-man/

Kelsky, K. (2017, October 15). The Professor Is In: 4 Steps to a Strong Tenure File. Retrieved from https://www.chronicle.com/article/The-Professor-Is-In-4-Steps/241451

Kenton. (n.d.). bias definition. Retrieved from https://sociologydictionary.org/bias/

Kessler, G. (2015, June 16). The stale statistic that one in three black males 'born today' will end up in jail. Retrieved from https://www.washingtonpost.com/news/fact-checker/wp/2015/06/16/the-stale-statistic-that-one-in-three-black-males-has-a-chance-of-ending-up-in-jail/?utm_term=.1f1d54ee89e1

Kimberlé Crenshaw on Intersectionality, More than Two Decades Later. (2017, June 8). Retrieved from https://www.law.columbia.edu/pt-br/news/2017/06/kimberle-crenshaw-intersectionality

Mogilevsky, M. (2016, December 19). 5 Ways Christian Privilege Shows Up During the Winter Holiday Season. Retrieved from https://everydayfeminism.com/2015/12/christian-privilege-holidays/

Mrs. Clinton Campaign Speech. (1996, January 25). Retrieved from https://www.c-span.org/video/?69606-1/mrs-clinton-campaign-speech

Murray-García, J., & Tervalon, M. (2017). Rethinking intercultural competence. *Intercultural Competence in Higher Education,* 19-31. doi:10.4324/9781315529257-3

North Dakota Cedar & Sage: Retrieved from:

https://und.edu/student-life/housing/_files/docs/sagesweetgrass.pdf

Paul, K. (2018, August 05). America's 1% hasn't controlled this much wealth since before the Great Depression. Retrieved from https://www.marketwatch.com/story/wealth-inequality-in-the-us-is-almost-as-bad-as-it-was-right-before-the-great-depression-2018-07-19

Rubin, J., John, P. S., Esquivel, P., & Queally, J. (2017, November 29). How a U.S. citizen was mistakenly targeted for deportation. He's not alone. Retrieved from https://www.latimes.com/local/lanow/la-me-ice-citizen-arrest-20171129-story.html

Social Justice Advocacy. (n.d.). Retrieved from http://equity.psu.edu/social-justice

Spencer, Herbert (1898) *The principles of sociology*. D. Appleton and Company, New York.

The Lucifer Effect: Understanding How Good People Turn Evil, Zimbardo (2007)

TED. (2016, December 07). The urgency of intersectionality | Kimberlé Crenshaw. Retrieved from https://www.youtube.com/watch?v=akOe5-UsQ2o

The Story: An Overview of the Experiment. (n.d.). Retrieved from https://www.prisonexp.org/the-story

Tolle, E. (2005). A New Earth: Awakening to your life's' purpose. New York, NY: Penguin Group.

U.S. and World Population Clock. (n.d.). Retrieved from https://www.census.gov/popclock

Utt, J. (2018). Series On: Systemic Whiteness

Vagins, D. J. (n.d.). The Simple Truth about the Gender Pay Gap. Retrieved from https://www.aauw.org/research/the-simple-truth-about-the-gender-pay-gap/

Jane Coaston, 2019 https://www.vox.com/the-highlight/2019/5/20/18542843/intersectionality-conservatism-law-race-gender-discrimination

Waters, A., & Asbill, L. (2013, August). Reflections on Cultural Humility. Retrieved from https://www.apa.org/pi/families/resources/newsletter/2013/08/cultural-humility.aspx

Glossary/Key Terms

This list is designed to offer diversity, equity, and inclusion practitioners and learners access to a set of common terms reflective of social justice work. *It is not meant to be exhaustive.* Visceral Change acknowledges that language evolves, and encourages you to continue learning, growing, and listening to the beauty of differences.

Ableism: The oppressive set of beliefs or practices that devalue and discriminate against people with physical, intellectual, or psychiatric disabilities; often referred to as "visible" or "invisible" disabilities.

Cisgender: Denoting a person whose gender expression and identity corresponds with the social expectations of their biological sex.

Conscious: Demonstrating a political commitment to deep, intentional engagement with and understanding of history, social and cultural issues and events; can relate to mindfulness and morality; may take the form of activism and intellect.

Diversity: The active appreciation of difference and differences often related to marginalized identities.

Dominant (Identity): Identities that receive major social privilege, power, or capital; generally reinforced through normalization.

Equity: Quality of being fair/fair-minded and justice oriented.

Gender Expression: The ways in which an individual presents their gender through cultural or social identifiers such as hair styles, clothing, and body language.

Gender Identity: The way in which a person identifies as it relates to their gender; often indicated through pronouns.

Genderqueer/Genderfluid: A term used to acknowledge a person who does not identify as a man or woman in order to reject gender as a binary and recognize it as a fluid blend of sexually assigned traditions and customs.

Heteronormativity: The systemic construct that advantages heterosexual norms and behaviors and disadvantages non-heterosexual norms and behaviors by assuming heterosexuality as standard, correct, or acceptable.

Inclusion: The active incorporation and meaningful involvement of all identities, often related to marginalized identities.

Inclusive Excellence: Best practices for maximizing the intersection of diversity and inclusion as a means to operate an organization in the most equitable way possible.

Intersectionality: The recognition that people are made up of multiple identities and that their marginal or privileged status is often a result of the "both/and" not the "either/or." Original term coined by feminist, legal scholar, Kimberle Crenshaw (1989) to address race and gender.

Marginalized: A term used to describe individuals or groups whose (subordinated) identities have granted them less privileges and opportunities in a given context; i.e. those 'on the margins' or sidelines of society.

Native Language Learner: Individuals, generally through nationalization or birth-right, who fluently speak the dominant language of their culture, environment, or society.

Native Language Speaker: Individuals who learn the dominant language of their or culture, environment, or society.

People of Color: Racial designation for any persons who identify with a race other than White or Caucasian.

Privilege: A term recognizing the systemic construct that grants or rescinds benefits and advantages to certain social identities based on their dominant or subordinated status.

Racism: A belief or doctrine that inherent differences among various human racial groups determine cultural or individual achievement; usually fostered by policies, systems of government, etc.

Social Identity: One's sense of self as a member of a social group or groups.

Subordinated (Identity): Identities that receive little to no social privilege, power, or capital.

Systemic Oppression: A series of discriminatory practices, policies, or procedures systemically designed to oppress a specific sect of people or persons.

A DIAMOND IS A DIAMOND

Transgender: Denoting or relating to a person whose sense of personal identity and gender does not correspond with their birth sex.

Transracial: The placing of a child from one racial or ethnic group with adoptive parents of another racial or ethnic group.

Made in the USA
Las Vegas, NV
19 August 2021